OLD MONEY STYLE

ACORN STREET PRESS

Interior Layout: MartinPublishingServices.com

ISBN: 978-1-950118-05-2 (hardback), 978-1-950118-04-5 (paperback)

OLD MONEY STYLE

Secrets to Dressing Well for Less

THE GENTLEMAN'S EDITION

BYRON TULLY

ACORN STREET PRESS

CONTENTS

Introduction

If you've received this book as a gift, thank the person who gave it to you: they obviously care about you and want the best for you.

If you've purchased this book for yourself, congratulations. Clearly you want to improve the your personal style and gain new insights into how that can be accomplished.

So let's discuss style at the outset, and get a very clear picture of what it is, where it comes from, and what it requires.

Style refers to a distinctive overall appearance or look that has a definite, purposeful design. This design conveys, from the wearer, a nonverbal message that is consistent, even if it may not be always obvious to the observer. In this context, the purpose of style is to be persuasive. To be effective, it should be timeless.

You may have suspected that true style cannot be lifted from photos in a fashion magazine. It can't be purchased off the shelf in a boutique, appropriated from the logos on a brand of clothing, or created by a designer, no matter how talented or inspired. It cannot, sadly, even be acquired from reading a book. However, relevant, well-presented information can lead you to developing your own style, which is the purpose of this book.

True style conforms to certain traditions, but is free of hard-and-fast rules. It is, at its zenith, noticed by others slowly if at all, and appreciated afterwards for quite some time. This is because of where it comes from and what it communicates.

True style originates in the character of the person. It is, as has been noted, the 'dress of thought'. Style is a natural expression of the self, of one's self-image, one's beliefs, and one's aspirations.

Style is not something that you put on only when you go out, dressed for the public. It is something you embody, at home, in private, even in what the poets call 'the midnight of your soul'.

The truth is that 'style' does not require spending money. More than anything else, it requires awareness, understanding, and forethought. You must adopt a philosophy, a perspective, and an attitude to fully inform the garments you wear. These combined elements—the philosophy, the perspective, and the attitude—are essential to Old Money Style.

The benefits of understanding this style—the manner of dress and behavior preferred and practiced by the world's Upper Class—will be numerous. You'll be relieved to know that you can dress well and look good without a lot of expense and with minimal effort. You'll make the people you care about happy because you took the time to look good and dress appropriately. Your confidence will reign supreme because your attire and demeanor will more accurately reflect your abilities and values.

Information brings awareness, and awareness—embraced and applied—opens the door to style and sophistication. In this context, 'sophistication' is not being outfitted with the latest, but being comfortable with the timeless.

The combination of style information, style awareness, and style understanding can give you a clearer, broader picture of how to dress in order to become a far more interesting gentleman than the average Joe. All of this simply requires a willingness to learn.

If a man neglects the opportunity to learn—in a classroom, in daily life, or from a book—he runs the risk of remaining uneducated, uninformed, and immature. He can appear to be uncaring, when in actuality he may simply be unaware.

Information is available to everyone. Seek it out in your continuing efforts to improve your style.

WHAT THIS BOOK IS AND HOW TO USE IT

This book is a reference guide. It is for men who want to learn the fundamentals of dressing well quickly, in an easy-to-understand and straightforward format that can be referred to again and again over the years.

This book is for the modern man, the young man, the seasoned man, the aspirational man. It can help anyone identify and source quality items and build an enduring, classic wardrobe that will last a lifetime.

I suggest that you read the book all the way through at least once. This will allow you to enjoy it without undue pressure, and allow you to be introduced in a general way to the philosophy and coding of Old Money Style.

Return to appropriate chapters and review them as you prepare to enhance your wardrobe, piece by piece, over time. You may also want to return to certain chapters that articulate this philosophy and code to help you embrace it as you go forward in life.

WHY I WROTE THIS BOOK

It is my intention to help you be your best self.

It's my intention to provide you with tools to help *increase your income* by showing you how to present yourself professionally and confidently to your clients and colleagues.

It's my intention to provide you with tools to help you *save more money* by showing you how to curate quality pieces, buy fewer clothes, and buy clothes less often.

It's my intention to provide you with tools to help you *garner respect* by showing you how to combine your garments for maximum (but subtle) visual impact, and help you avoid looking out of date, out of touch, ridiculous, or worse.

It's my intention to provide you with tools to help you *be more attractive* to potential sex partners, business partners, and life partners.

If you care about any of these things, read on.

If you don't care about these things, perhaps it's time you did. So, read on.

WHAT THIS BOOK IS, AND IS NOT

This is a blueprint, not an encyclopedia.

There are hundreds of (usually huge) books that provide insights into the rich history of men's clothing. They show beautiful photos of well-dressed men through the decades and provide volumes of information about how men have dressed well in the past and how men can dress well today.

Many of these books are written by well-informed authors who are passionate about the subtly of a houndstooth check fabric, the shoulder construction of a Neapolitan jacket, or the relative merits of a forward pleat.

You will not find that in this book. You will find a definite perspective, a cadre of time-tested fundamentals, and a proven list of vendors. These can act as a map, a constellation of sorts to guide you through this new way of thinking.

However you choose to explore this new frontier, it is important that you explore it. Do your own independent research and study. Discover timeless elements. Form your own opinions. Develop your own personal style, a style that is a reflection of the man you are now, and the man you aspire to become.

Be curious. Investigate. Learn. This process will help you absorb and apply the knowledge presented here in the most effective way possible: through explanation, exercise, engagement, and example.

What My Perspective Is, And Is Not

I write about the values, priorities, and habits of Old Money, people who've had wealth and privilege for 3 generations or more. So my perspective, influenced both by observation and background, leans toward the traditional rather than the trendy, to the functional over the fashionable, to the enduring over the transient.

With that in mind, I'm going to encourage you to dress—and live—as follows:

- in a manner that's going to age well;
- in a manner that's going to serve you well in terms of style and comfort;
- in a manner that expresses respect for yourself, for others, for the daily obligations you have, and for the events you attend;
- in a manner that's going to allow you to look back with pride, or at least without embarrassment, upon *the way* in which you conducted yourself.

I'm not suggesting you 'dress preppy', but if you did, it wouldn't be the worst thing in life.

I'm simply going to ask that you give your clothing some direction, some definition, and some purpose. In summary, I'm going to strongly recommend that you give your clothes not some, but a lot of thought.

Why? Because other people give your clothes a lot of thought, even if they or you are not aware of it. They judge you by your clothes and how you wear them. They notice whether or not your clothes are in good condition. They notice what you wear and when you wear it. By that I mean how you're dressed for a particular occasion, and how you dress every day.

It may not be fair, but it's always been this way and it will always be this way. Best to accept it, adapt to it, and take advantage of it. A gentleman's wardrobe should be well-thought-out and focused.

Your Choices: Past, Present, and Future

Whether you admit it or realize it, you wear the clothes you wear right now for a reason, beyond simply protecting your body from the elements. In the same way that you would be making a statement if you walked naked in the street, you are making a statement by the clothes you wear out in public each day.

You may say, 'I just dress to be comfortable', or 'This is all I can afford', but, most likely, there's more to your choices than these easy excuses can dismiss or conceal.

I'm not a psychologist. I can only share what I have experienced about clothes and people. You may need to figure out why you're not presenting yourself as best you can and address that.

It may be that you're dressing the way everyone in your family has always dressed, or you're rebelling against that. It may be that you're dressing the way your peer group dresses in order to fit in and be accepted by them. It may also be possible that you simply have not been exposed to the basics of dressing well, and you're just winging it with influences from fashion magazines or television.

With new information, your perception of how clothing impacts your life may change, and you may change your choices as a result of that.

If you have never thought of these things, think of them now. If you want to ensure that your clothes are an advantage and an asset in life rather than a disadvantage and a liability, keep an open mind and consider some fundamentals I'm going to introduce.

It's inevitable that you're going to spend money on clothes. Spend it wisely. You have choices about the clothes you wear. Choose wisely. You communicate to others through what you wear. Communicate wisely.

The information and principles presented in this book have worked for generations of men in the past, and they'll serve all of us well going forward.

Let's get to it.

Part I

Perspective

THE PHILOSOPHY BEHIND YOUR WARDROBE

Why talk about a philosophy of dressing well?

The answer is simple: if we understand 'why' something is the way it is, or does what it does, it's easier to digest it, personalize it, and implement it.

Functionally, clothing protects us from the elements—rain, cold, the blazing sun, mosquitos—and keeps us from getting arrested for indecent exposure.

Everything else clothing does, from that basic task forward, is psychological. Remember that.

We use clothing to express ourselves, to communicate, to provoke, and possibly to control or influence the behavior of others, or even ourselves.

Our choice of clothing impacts our daily experiences. For example:

- You may wear a jacket to support your local sports team, identifying and bonding with your 'tribe';
- You may be required by your company or boss to dress a certain way in order to appear professional in the workplace for the benefit of your clients and colleagues;
- You may have noticed that children behave better when they're dressed up (ask any teacher on class photo day);
- You may get better service at restaurants and shops when you dress well; and
- You may even feel better about yourself when you dress well.

William Shakespeare, the greatest playwright in history, said, "Clothes maketh the man."

Smart people have known these truths for a long time.

THE UNIFORM

Napoleon Bonaparte, one of the greatest generals of all time, noted that, "A man becomes a creature of his uniform."

So let's talk about a uniform that can work for you.

The 'uniform' that we're going to use as a North Star is based on a combination of two sartorial traditions: the prep school uniforms worn by students at private schools in New England, and the no-nonsense style of Old Money Guys living in Boston.

These wardrobe concepts are solid, timeless, and universally effective. We honor these two prototypes because of the values they represent:

- education and equality: every student in a prep school wears in the same uniform, and gets the same education, regardless of whether they're rich or poor; and
- function and modesty: season after season, Old Money Guys in Boston wear quality clothes that look good, but don't obviously call attention to their wealth or position in their community.

We also honor them for their simplicity. The prep school student is most often attired in his blue blazer, rep tie, white or blue shirt, with khakis or grey slacks. The Old Money Guy has his go-to tweed jacket, comfortable sweater, dress shirt, warm pants, and sturdy shoes. Nothing fancy. Nothing frilly.

Both the student and the OMG wear what works. They wear what's appropriate for their position and their duties. They don't have to think about it too much. (Admittedly, the prep school student doesn't get to think about their uniform at all: they're just told to put it on and get their ass to class.)

THE PROCESS

There is a process I propose you go through in order to create your uniform. I encourage you to take the following steps:

- learn the importance of quality clothing and what it communicates;
- prioritize garments you wear daily to make the most of your budget;
- assemble a balanced inventory of go-to pieces;
- preserve and protect your investment by organizing, cleaning, and storing your clothes properly;
- know the outfit that's appropriate for the occasion or the weather;
- dress each day without worry, confusion, or delay; and
- get on with life and living.

Remember: in this part of the book, I'm explaining why we dress the way we do and teaching you how to think about clothes. In the second part of this book, we'll explore an itemized inventory with detailed descriptions of those go-to pieces.

This two-step approach will help you build a wardrobe over time that is:

- traditional in style;
- high in quality;
- reasonable in price;
- versatile in use;
- durable in construction; and
- modest in presentation.

All this, without thinking about it too much, but still with an understanding of what you're doing and why.

Now, let's talk about what your wardrobe is supposed to do…

THE PURPOSE OF YOUR WARDROBE

Historically, the purpose of a woman's wardrobe has been to appear desirable. You can discuss and debate among yourselves how much or how little this has changed.

Ideally, the purpose of a man's wardrobe is to appear reliable. Do not think for one second that this has changed. 'Can I count on you?' This is one of the great questions in life, central to every human relationship. This is what your partner wants to know. This is what your boss wants to know. This is what your employees want to know. This is what your friends and family want to know.

Present an image of reliability—as someone who honors his commitments, fulfills his responsibilities, and is present emotionally—in the way you dress. Then follow up that presentation with performance—in the way you act.

Dressing to impress is a mistake. Avoid the peacock syndrome: trying to desperately garner attention through flamboyant attire. Avoid the imposter syndrome: trying to appear wealthier than you really are. Anyone you really want to impress can spot a phony a mile away.

Remember the purpose of your wardrobe as you dress for every occasion.

Random Rule: it should take five minutes for someone to realize you are well-dressed. That is how subtle your clothing should be.

When you dress, you are communicating. People will see you, assess you, make an educated guess about your background, conclude that you have certain character traits, assume you have certain abilities, and decide if they want to get to know you before you ever say a word.

All this is determined largely by the style of dress you've adopted. All this happens very quickly, according to psychologists, who estimate this analysis can take about 3 seconds.

Biased? Oh, yes. Likely to continue? Oh, yes.

LIGHTS...CAMERA...WARDROBE!

Think about this: the same visual process I just described occurs when you're watching a movie. A character enters a scene, and you, the viewer, see him for the first time. If you were experiencing this story as a novel, with written words on the page, the author might take a page and a half to tell you about this character: who is he, where he's from, what he wants, and a description of what he looks like.

A film director doesn't have that much time: the character must be visually communicated to you, the viewer, in seconds.

How does the director do that? She doesn't, actually. A costume designer has been hired do that. The costume designer reads the script, figures out that this character is, let's say, the villain. The designer then finds the right wardrobe for that character so that, when the audience sees the character, they instantly get a good idea of who he is and how he might fit into the film's story.

So when you see John Malkovich enter a scene wearing a warm-up suit, a shiny T-shirt, and a gold chain around his neck, you think, Oh, there's John Malkovich, I love that guy. Subconsciously, you also think: in an outfit like that, he's probably the bad guy, because only gangsters wear track suits, silk T-shirts, and gold chains.

In fact, if a guy wears a gold chain in a movie it almost always means he's a gangster. It can be subtle, like the loan shark in *Michael Clayton* who barely had his dangling over his sweater collar, or obvious, like Al Pacino in *Scarface*. But that's the way it is.

Conversely, if you see a movie character wearing a tan corduroy jacket, that character is a journalist. Watch *All the President's Men* with Robert Redford, from the 1970s, or Ewan McGregor in the more recent film *Miles Ahead*, the Miles Davis biopic. Tan corduroy jacket equals journalist.

This process is how visual psychology works. It is important to understand this so you can use it to your benefit.

People are going to frame your 'character' in their mind when they see the way you've dressed. This is your first opportunity to shape their perception and make a good impression.

Of course, whether the speech and action that follow that first impression matches their assumptions in terms of character and competence is completely up to you. But the clothing is the starting point that we're addressing here.

R-E-S-P-E-C-T

The way you dress tells the world who you are, who you want to be, how much you respect yourself, and how they can treat you.

Everybody wants to be treated with respect. The way you dress contributes—one way or another—to the odds of you consistently getting that respect. The mistakes men make in choosing their clothes most often come from, first, not realizing that clothes are a part of the 'respect' equation, and, second, by failing to understand and adhere to a basic 'code' of dressing well.

When you watch a world-class athlete perform, you are obviously watching God-given talent in action. Talent, and a lot of discipline, of course.

What you may be less aware of is the fact that you are watching someone execute the fundamentals of their chosen sport very, very well. Apply that analogy to clothing, execute the fundamentals of dressing well, and you'll enjoy world-class results from your wardrobe.

My goal here is to articulate and share these fundamentals. Your job is to understand the fundamentals and implement them in your daily life.

Note: simply changing your clothing is not going to change your character or your life. You must adopt and adhere to 'values'—principles that you think are important—to change your behavior, which will then alter the quality of your life. Clothing is a small but important part of this process.

STYLE VS. FASHION

You will, of course, avoid fashion like the plague. 'Fashion' is the industry that markets new garments to consumers at least 4 times a year, changing for every season. These new garments are proclaimed to be 'the latest trend', the 'must have' items that only people 'in the know' will be wearing. Don't buy it. Literally. Don't buy it. Don't buy fashionable clothes.

Instead, focus on 'style'. Style is, very simply, the overall message you communicate with your clothes.

The style is comfortable. It incorporates natural fabrics like wool, cotton, and linen. Actually, it uses only those three fabrics—100% cotton, 100% wool, 100% linen—with a little silk, which is used for neckties, and a little synthetic fabric for the odd waterproof winter coat.

The style is moderate. This means that the cut on your garments is not too loose and it is not too tight. The shoulders of your jackets are 'natural', not too padded. The lapels are not too wide and not too narrow. The cut of your pants and shirts is not too short and not too long.

The style is subdued. The predominant colors are blue, brown, tan, and grey for most of your suits, jackets, and dress pants. White and blue for your shirts. A rainbow of colors can be thrown in on sweaters, ties, scarves, and casual pants. Your shoes are usually brown.

The style is traditional. This means it hasn't changed much and won't change much. You can purchase classic, quality garments, wear them and take care of them, replace them slowly over time, and look absolutely fantastic for decades.

The style is Old Money Style. Congratulations. This is your style.

THE INVESTMENT MINDSET

Purchase each article of clothing as an investment. An investment is something that is intended to provide *more value over time than the price paid to acquire it.*

Here are some factors you might consider as you devise an investment strategy for your wardrobe.

Frequency: it's best to invest first in the clothes that you're most likely to wear every day: shirts, shoes, pants, jackets. These are the garments you 'need'. Then go down the list to other garments that you wear less often, or seasonally, like a winter coat or a tuxedo.

Quality: it's best to invest in quality garments because they last longer and are better investments over time than cheap garments. People will, more often than not, notice your shirt and your shoes more than anything else. Prioritize quality over cost on those two, as it's difficult to hide a poorly made shirt, and it quickly becomes painful to walk in poorly made shoes.

Quantity: it's best to invest in pieces that are versatile, i.e. those that can used for different occasions and with different outfits. Investing in this way, you purchase fewer items overall. You purchase higher quality items and in doing so enjoy garments that last longer. So you'll replace them less often.

Value: it's best to calculate the value—as well as the price—of each item. Let's say you've got your eye on a blue blazer. You'll weigh the price of it against the look and durability of the fabric and construction, how often you're going to use it, and how long you expect it to last. The price is what you pay. The value is what you get.

If you're going to spend $800.00 to buy a traditionally-styled, well-made, name-brand blue blazer that you're going to wear to work frequently, to dinners out regularly, and to weddings every once in a while, for the next ten years, that's a good investment.

Going forward, this is how you're going to look at the acquisition of clothes. Strategically, thoughtfully, deliberately, logically.

Again: How often am I going to wear this? How much does it cost? How long will it last?

Remember: the 'How long will it last?' question actually means two things: How durable is the garment itself? and, How timeless is the style?

These are the hard questions to ask yourself as you consider a purchase, but hard questions and honest answers lead to good decisions.

TERMS AND CONDITIONS

There are terms we'll use in discussing your wardrobe which may not be new to you, but which I'll nevertheless clarify below. Some refer to how garments are made, and also include some professionals you'll work with to keep your clothes and shoes in good condition. Some, like the iron and ironing board, are familiar, and are presented as options to consider.

OFF THE RACK

As the phrase implies, this refers to clothing that you will purchase 'as is', off of the hanger in a store, or from a website. With 'off the rack' pants or suits, alterations may be required, but the time and costs involved with these are usually minimal. (Cuffs on pants, length on jacket sleeves, not a big deal.)

Most of your wardrobe will be composed of items you have purchased 'off the rack' and will work perfectly fine, if you know what to buy and where to buy it. We'll cover these details in the second part of the book.

MADE TO MEASURE

This term refers to a process by which you are sized by a tailor, usually using a garment you already own, to approximate the dimensions of a new garment. This new garment will be measured, cut, and constructed for you personally, but will not be completely tailored for every unique characteristic of your body. It may fit you better than an 'off the rack' garment, especially if you are very tall, very short, or very thin, but it won't be what is often referred to as 'custom made' or 'bespoke' clothing.

Made-to-measure sometimes costs more than off the rack, sometimes not, and allows you to have more say about the fabric and cut of your clothes. Made-to-measure dress shirts are common purchases for men who want their dress shirts to fit a little better than the ones on offer in department stores or online, even if they still wear off the rack suits, jackets, and pants.

Bespoke

This term is used to describe the particular experience of entering a tailor's shop and having a garment made especially for you. The tailor takes a number of measurements of your body, offers you a number of fabrics and styles to choose from, and proceeds through a number of fittings to ensure that the garment you've purchased fits you, and only you, like a glove, incorporating all of your preferences.

Bespoke is a term most often used to refer to suits and jackets, but shirts, pants, and shoes can also be categorized as bespoke.

Unless you have a real passion for clothes, a real need to look very, very well dressed, a real understanding of the craftsmanship involved, and a real big, fat wallet to work with, bespoke is not something to concern yourself with right now.

The Tailor

An experienced alterations tailor is the one person who can help you achieve a 'made-to-measure' or even 'bespoke' look with your 'off the rack' garments.

They can do this very economically by altering your well-thought-out purchases—a little here and a little there—to make them fit you well. They'll shorten the sleeves on a jacket or hem the cuffs on a pair of pants for not very much money, and in just a few days.

They will also be able to repair damaged fabric, replace lost buttons, or replicate and replace collars and cuffs on worn shirts.

You may find a good alterations tailor with a good eye at your local dry cleaners, or you may find them with their own shop, where they do alterations or even create bespoke clothing for clients.

As you assemble your wardrobe, find the alterations tailor who can add value to your clothes without a lot of added expense.

THE IRON AND THE IRONING BOARD

One of the choices you have when you begin the upgrading process is this: do I buy 100% cotton dress shirts and commit to ironing them? Or do I fall back on buying 'non-iron' or 'Perma-Press' shirts that I can just pull out of the washer or dryer, put on a hanger, and wear when I'm ready?

The look of a freshly ironed shirt is superior to a non-iron shirt, in my opinion. And there are chemicals in non-iron shirt fabrics that you may not want to be exposed to. So keep that in mind. It is tempting to go with the no-iron option, and you will not be condemned to the depths of hell if you do.

To efficiently handle the ironing chore for the shirts that need it, take a few minutes on Sunday afternoon, iron all of your shirts for the week, hang them in your closet, and be ready to roll on Monday morning.

THE DRY CLEANERS AND THE LAUNDRY

If you choose to send your garments to a dry cleaners, make sure you find a good vendor in your area. Bad dry cleaning damages your investment.

If you choose to send your shirts to a dry cleaners or commercial laundry to have them washed and pressed, expect them to not look as nice as they would had you ironed them yourself.

Time and money are the trade-offs. Choose wisely.

THE SHOE REPAIR GUY

Few pieces in a man's wardrobe are more important than his shoes. It may be cliché but you really can tell a lot about a man from the kind of shoes he wears, their quality, and their condition.

A man who truly knows what he's doing—protecting his investment and making a good impression—will know the importance of a cobbler, or shoe repair person, the craftsman who maintains and repairs shoes.

There's probably one in your neighborhood. Probably near the dry cleaners. Find a good shoe repair shop. Your shoes may be one of your biggest investments. They should last at least ten years and perhaps twenty.

If you live in a pedestrian city (New York, Boston, London, Rome, or Paris) and walk or take public transportation to and from work, you're going to visit a cobbler more than someone driving a car back and forth to work.

The heels on your shoes will wear out first and more often than anything else. Then the soles will start to wear out. The last part or your shoes that should wear out is the leather that everyone sees.

Keep your shoes polished. Do it yourself if you prefer, or let the cobbler polish them when he replaces or repairs the heels. If you walk in rain and snow, you can invest in some galoshes (rubber overshoes) that protect your dress shoes in the rain, snow, and slush.

Keeping your shoes in good condition is critical, both for the way you look and the well-being of your feet, legs, and lower back. Quality shoes can be old in years and traditional in style, but they need consistent attention in order to be an asset to you.

If you purchase your shoes from Allen Edmonds (a vendor I recommend) you can look into their 'recrafting service' as your shoes begin to show wear.

GARMENT STORAGE AND PRESERVATION

To keep your wool and cashmere clothes in good condition and increase their lifespan, store them in canvas garment bags during the spring and summer. Avoid plastic. The clothes can't breathe in plastic. Excess moisture can contribute to mould, mildew, staining, and discoloration of fabric.

Moths are the enemy of your wool garments. They can lay 50 to 1000 eggs at a time, and the ideal diet for these little bastard larvae is wool, cashmere, silk, angora, and fur. Generally they lay their eggs in dark, enclosed, and undisturbed places. The larva feed off of the wool—your wool jacket, coat, or pants, for example—as they grow into moths. Their feeding can and will leave holes in and destroy your garments. Quite rude, but good to know.

Moth balls are a chemical product that keep moths away from garments. Historically they were made of camphor, a waxy, white or clear substance made most often from the camphor laurel. The balls don't smell very good and can be discouraging to moths. This smell can also be discouraging to human beings, so use them as a last resort.

Know that moth-eaten garments are not something you want to wear in public. Skilled artisans who repair this kind of damage are readily available, but can be expensive.

Preservation of your investment (your clothes) is key. Again, the best option is to keep your garments stored safely in canvas garment bags, out of the reach of moths and the glare of sunlight, which can fade the color of the fabric.

To protect the shape of your garments, purchase good quality wooden hangers. Wood is a sturdy, organic material. It will not warp or bend over time.

Keep a dozen in your closet at home, and keep one or two in your office for your wool coat, blazer or jacket. Avoid using the backs of chairs, door knobs or hooks. Wooden hangers are best. Invest in them as you go forward.

THE RETAIL LANDSCAPE

The term 'retail landscape' refers to the sources you explore in order to find your clothes.

This includes men's stores, department stores, vintage stores, and online stores. Here is a quick overview of what to expect in terms of products, prices, and experiences at each.

THE MEN'S STORE

This is a brick-and-mortar men's clothing store that only sells clothing. Walmart is not a men's clothing store. In an authentic men's clothing store, the man who greets you and helps you select garments may also be the owner. He may also be a tailor, but he'll most likely have a tailor on staff or on call. The store generally focuses on one style of clothes—traditional or trendy—and makes personal service and professional advice part of its value package.

If you look at the person who greets you and waits on you at, say, Brooks Brothers, you can derive a certain amount of confidence and comfort knowing that he is probably dressed well. He will probably dress you well if you allow him to advise you.

At an authentic men's clothing store, the selection may be limited to the store's own product or a curated selection of kindred brands that fit within the store's wheelhouse. That's okay. You aren't interested in a wide variety of styles. You're interested in Old Money Style, good quality, good advice, and in-house tailoring services. You will pay for these, but it will be worth it.

If you completely lose your entire mind and decide to go to a trendy store in a mall, remember: you will be exposed to fashion, not style. You may be given advice, not by an proprietor who understands and appreciates sartorial traditions, but rather by a 'sales associate' who may be working on commission, or just employed for the summer. The advice may be sketchy. The quality of the merchandise may be random. Most likely, only the prices will be attractive. Your goal is style, not fashion.

Move on.

THE DEPARTMENT STORE

The beauty of the Department Store is that it has a large variety of men's clothing brands in a range of price points and quality standards. These stores have to move their merchandise on a regular schedule in order to make room for the next season's products. Often they have mid-year or end-of-year sales.

During these sales, you can pick up some great pieces for not very much money. Get to know a reliable person in the men's department in order to get a heads-up on sales dates. Buy 'off season', i.e., wool sweaters in spring, cotton pants at the end of summer.

Once you've learned which brands and garments work for you, you can then loiter with intent until a big sale comes up, and snag your go-to items at a discounted price once or twice a year. This is commonly referred to as a plan. Remember: limit your poaching to only quality items that work for you, once or twice a year.

THE VINTAGE STORE

That's right. Don't be shocked. Old Money honors value and keeps it real. If you're just starting out or staring over, vintage stores—especially those adjacent to affluent neighborhoods—often have top quality, slightly or never-worn coats and jackets at rock bottom prices.

Buying shirts from vintage stores can be tricky, but sometimes overcoats, blazers, jackets, and ties are like new and priced to move.

Again, you should know which brands and garments work for you, and you should inspect each garment very carefully for stains, wear, and damage. You should also be aware of how the garment is cut: some jackets look fine until you look at the cut of the lapels and realize the jacket is obviously from the 1970s, and not in a good way. You don't want that.

What you're looking for in vintage stores, especially if you live in New York or Los Angeles, is a garment used as wardrobe in a movie, television show, or commercial that's been worn once or twice, if at all. It's like new, current in its traditional style, and undamaged. Search for quality, top-end brands.

If you live elsewhere, again, locate a vintage, charity, or thrift store near an affluent neighborhood. The guys who drop off their unwanted jackets and coats there probably dress Old Money Style, too.

Online shopping

The greatest benefit online shopping provides you is the convenience of never leaving your home (or work cubicle) and having your purchase delivered directly to your door. Again, once you have found which merchant sells the product that works for you, you can order the size and color of your choice with little to worry about.

Make certain you know the vendor. Read customer reviews. Ask around. Quality issues and return policies are the two main reasons to stick with reputable vendors and brands you trust. They have a reputation to protect, and you don't need the hassle that comes with poor service.

I recommend purchasing directly from a brand's homepage and dealing exclusively with their customer service people. (Brooks Brothers, LL Bean, Lands' End, Allen Edmonds, and Mercer and Sons Shirts are good examples of companies with solid track records in this area.)

Note: I refer to brands in this book, not as a way to convey status, but as a way to predict quality. You should look at them in this way also.

Also be aware that I do not receive any compensation from the brands I recommend. I'm an author, not an 'influencer'.

THE IMPACT OF CHEAP CLOTHING

It's tempting—and easy on your wallet—to bounce around town in a ten-dollar T-shirt, twenty-dollar cargo pants, and five-dollar flip-flops. You're getting really cheap clothing that serves the purpose. Right?

Not exactly. If you purchase an incredibly cheap garment, the retail store where you bought it made a profit. The wholesaler or manufacturer made a profit, as well, even after rent for their facilities, cost of materials, and wages for employees.

So, what is the quality of that cheap garment? How many washings will it survive? And most importantly, how much do you think they pay their employees to make a T-shirt that you can buy for ten dollars? The answer is: very little or nothing. What conditions do these employees work in? The answer is: almost always horrible.

Sometimes these people are prisoners or slaves. It is shocking to think that these working conditions still exist today, but they do. They are not just unfair, they are inhumane. When you purchase cheap clothes at 'unbeatable' prices, you are, very often, enabling this blood-stained industry to continue and flourish.

What can you do to not participate in this injustice? The answer is: don't buy cheap clothing. It's a waste of money: cheap stuff doesn't last. It simply perpetuates unjust labor conditions around the world.

Cheap clothing also gets thrown away quickly. It clogs landfills and places an unnecessary burden on the already-over taxed environment.

So, now you know.

Man up. Pay for quality clothes.

ONE DAY AT A TIME

I sincerely believe that most men want to look good when they go out to face the world each day. They want to put their best foot forward, for their families, for their careers, and for themselves.

To facilitate this, I've created easy-to-remember categories, pegged to your weekly routine and professional responsibilities. These categories provide direction on what to wear and how to wear it. It's a no-brainer, and you'll be well-dressed without even realizing it.

If you stick with the basic colors I suggest throughout the book and stay with Old Money Style garments, almost anything can be paired with almost anything, color and pattern wise, and look good.

Important note: if you are a plumber, carpenter, electrician, steelworker, truck driver, farmer, craftsman, landscape architect, technician, engineer, machinist, or mechanic, you may favor work clothes that can take the wear-and-tear, the sweat, the dirt, the oil, the heat, the cold, and the daily abuse that is part-and-parcel of the work you do every day. I get it, and I appreciate the way you keep our world running.

If you're a law enforcement officer, fireman, park ranger, or member of the armed services, you may wear a government-issued uniform when you're at work. Your attire is part of doing your job effectively and professionally, and I appreciate your efforts in keeping our world safe.

For men in these two groups, just take the categories below and implement them into your non-working hours. Not everyone can dress as they please while they're working. Everyone can, however, easily and effortlessly upgrade when you're spending time with the people you love, doing the things you enjoy, on your own time.

With the job, the kids, the soccer games, and the recitals, looking good shouldn't be another task to tack onto the to-do list. The way I've laid this out, it's simple. It's one less thing to think about, not one more thing to think about.

And it may give you that extra moment to remember to pick up flowers for that special someone on your way home.

So, with that said, let's detail your inventory. Here we go:

THE DAILY

The Daily covers a Monday through Friday, 9-to-5 routine, if you work in a 'business casual' office environment.

If you work in a 'jeans and t-shirt' office environment, consider The Daily as a way of elevating your look above that bare-minimum baseline.

In either case, you can comfortably rely on the following to treat you right:

- 100% cotton button-down dress shirt in blue or white, or one with thin blue and white stripes;
- a pair of 100% cotton pants (khakis maybe) in dark blue, olive green, brown, or a pair of grey or tan 100% wool slacks (simple brown belt);
- brown, grey, or navy blue socks, cotton or wool;
- brown dress shoes, which can be lace-ups, loafers, or chukka boots.

Add a solid color, 100% cotton or 100% wool crew-neck, V-neck, or cardigan sweater if it's chilly outside. Navy blue, dark green, grey, or burgundy are your go-to options.

And you're done.

THE DAILY JACKET

This category is for a slightly more dressed up office environment, an important lunch, an evening out, or cooler weather.

Take all of the above items included in the Daily and throw a blue blazer or tweed jacket on top. Yeah, it's that easy.

When you throw your jacket or blazer on, remember to fold and stuff a clean, white handkerchief in your exterior breast pocket, and keep another identical handkerchief in the interior pocket of your jacket or blazer at all times.

If you encounter a young lady in emotional distress, you'll gallantly reach inside your jacket, pull out your handkerchief, and offer it to her. She'll dry her tears, thank you profusely, and you'll be a hero. More likely, you'll just get the sniffles from the office air conditioning and need to wipe your nose discreetly.

Note: the Daily Jacket is the best way to travel. You'll be professional and comfortable. The layers of shirt, sweater, and jacket will give you options as the temperature changes from home to car to airport to airplane to new destination and back again.

If you pack a necktie, you'll be ready to do an easy 'wardrobe upgrade' if a slightly more elegant occasion arises while you're traveling.

The interior pockets on the jacket or blazer will also give you a safe place to put your wallet, travel documents, sunglasses, and phone.

THE DAILY DRESS

Take all of the above items, in any combination you choose, and add a 100% silk necktie to the look. That's the Daily Dress.

The necktie can be a blue, burgundy, or dark green, a rep tie with multicolored stripes, or a discreet pattern. If it's an evening event, go with a white shirt and solid color navy blue necktie to be a little more formal.

Indulge in pastel-colored neckties with the blue blazer for more formal events like church services, christenings, weddings, and fancy-schmancy country club soirees. Stripes or small patterns on neckties are fine for most occasions. A little color, but nothing too shiny or loud. Moderate width. The necktie is to be tied in a four-in-hand knot. (The tie knot will be discussed later.)

THE FORMAL

This ensemble revolves around the navy blue or grey business suit, the afore-mentioned white or blue dress shirt, and the afore-mentioned brown dress shoes.

(The term 'afore-mentioned' is important: it tells you that you're getting numerous uses out of a single garment, which is a good thing.)

You'll add the afore-mentioned 100% silk necktie to this outfit. A dark blue for more serious events. A white shirt and black necktie for memorial services.

Remember the white handkerchiefs in the breast pocket and interior pocket.

And you're done.

THE WEEKENDER

All week long, you've kept the stock market or the city's metro system from going off the rails, figuratively or literally. This is your time.

This is Saturday, Sunday, holidays—off the clock. Critical activities include coffee, croissants, newspaper, the college ballgame, silly cat videos on YouTube, bingeing on Netflix, or running to the grocery store for avocados, chips, and brew. Taking it easy. But still looking good.

You'll throw on the following comfortable, casual, but still confident pieces to look a cut above the average Joe:

- 100% cotton, solid color pullover polo shirt in navy blue, dark green, burgundy, or pink;
- the afore-mentioned cotton pants or khakis (maybe jeans) and a pair of the afore-mentioned loafers, Sperry Topsiders, or chukka boots;
- If the weather is chilly, throw the afore-mentioned dress shirt or sweater (or both!) over the polo shirt and keep warm.
- Wearing the socks and shaving the face, my good man, are optional.

If the weather is downright cold, you can layer up as you like, then throw a long wool coat or waterproof winter coat on top of all of it. (See our Inventory list in Part II for details on these coats, and all garments.)

SUMMARY OF PART I

In Part I, we've covered why you should dress well, what your clothes should do for you, and what you're facing as you look at purchasing clothes in the real world. We also touched on some basics about how to take care of your clothes and shoes.

We went through your (hypothetical) week, offering up options for your work, downtime, and special events. I've given you a solid, workable blueprint for what to throw on for each occasion.

Refer back to Part 1 of the book to remember why you're making the effort to improve your wardrobe, and what to wear when. After a while, all of this will be second nature. The only time you'll think about it is when somebody mentions how well dressed you always seem to be.

This is your life, your routine, and the clothes you wear with each to look good. Simple, comfortable, appropriate, and easy. Old Money Style.

Enjoy the experience.

In Part II, I'm going to itemize the inventory of garments you'll acquire and provide some details about each to help you make good choices as you go forward.

Here we go…

Part II

Inventory

Inventory

This section details the garments you'll need, who sells them, the approximate price range, when to wear them, and how to wear them.

We'll start with the most important, most frequently worn essentials and go down the list from there.

Don't feel compelled to go out and buy every item on this list immediately.

Think about your work situation, your goals, your lifestyle, and the climate you live in.

Determine how well the garments you already own will accommodate the Old Money Style garments you're going to acquire. Pretty well? Or not at all? Or some here, some there?

Research the inventory items online. Compare styles and prices of the vendors I offer up. Make some mental notes.

Decide on some priorities: do I need a couple of shirts first? The right shoes? Or a blue blazer?

Look at your budget: how much can you spend? Look at your calendar: how soon do you need it? Let the dust settle. Make some smart choices. Ease into the upgrade.

As you deliberately and strategically purchase new items, integrate the existing items you already have into your rotation if they work.

Give the other outdated and underperforming garments to charity.

Keep your closet and your life uncluttered.

THE STARTING FIVE

Before we hit the Inventory in item-by-item detail, I'm going to give you a nuts and bolts, down and dirty, bare minimum line-up of five garments that will serve you well, cradle to grave.

These are five important garments that form the pillars of a classic Old Money Style wardrobe. They will effectively (and inexpensively) communicate a positive image to others, whether these people consciously realize it or not.

Note: to more sophisticated and affluent people, these wardrobe basics convey the idea that you have at least a passing familiarity with the rules of civilized society. They must, however, be accompanied by manners.

These Old Money stalwarts will be the star players on your team. Fittingly, we're going to refer to them as The Starting Five.

By prioritizing these, you can quickly and inexpensively assemble a go-to outfit that will work for job interviews, business meetings, family gatherings, and happy hours. If you stick with these, you'll always look respectable, surprisingly sophisticated, and stylish.

The Starting Five are traditional, functional, versatile, and timeless.

They are:
- the navy blue blazer;
- the oxford cloth long sleeve button down dress shirt;
- khaki pants;
- brown lace-up dress shoes, loafers, or chukka boots; and
- a rep tie.

If you're on a tight budget and need to get an interview look together quickly, this is your list. If you just sold your tech company for $20 million and you're going to visit your girlfriend's parents, this is your list.

Why? Because if you go with the Starting Five, nobody will know how much money you have or don't have. (And you will never discuss it.) They'll only know that you're smart enough to dress well. You'll make a good first impression. Let them guess about the rest.

You should be aware that a lot of young guns just starting out with little or nothing, and a lot of Old Money Guys born with eight-figure trust funds, dress in pretty much the same manner: they turn to—and stay with—the Starting Five for their wardrobe fundamentals.

Everything I'm going to discuss in terms of Inventory going forward will expand on the Starting Five, the pillars of Old Money Style.

So let's get into the weeds and look at what every guy needs…

JACKETS AND SUITS

THE BLUE BLAZER

Description: 100% wool fabric with a silky smooth full lining, this jacket is generally immune to wrinkles and the odd spillage of beverages. Perhaps the most important garment in your wardrobe because it's versatile, durable, timeless, comfortable, and looks good on everyone.

History, if you care: alleged origins of the blue blazer are numerous, and none strain the bounds of credibility: a sea captain wanted to upgrade the look of his shabbily dressed crew and ordered uniform blue jackets for each and every one of them; a rivalry between Cambridge rowing clubs took a sartorial curve and transformed a red jacket (the original 'blazer', so named for its bright color) to a dark blue; or that the blazer was somehow the brilliant idea of Queen Victoria of England in the mid 1800s.

The blazer, in pretty much the same style we all know and wear today, hit American shores in the 1930s, with Brooks Brothers introducing it. Since then, the blue blazer has enjoyed unwavering popularity, immune to the hands of time and the winds of change.

It is one of the few garments that looks pretty much the same, regardless of the era in which it was constructed, or by the company or designer who made it.

It has remained a favorite of the well-dressed man for almost 200 years and remains an essential to any wardrobe inventory.

Common colors & fabrics: navy blue (duh), 100% wool gabardine.

Construction details: a natural, soft shoulder with a minimum of padding is best. Make sure the blazer is fully lined for easy on, easy off against your cotton dress shirt. Unlined or half-lined blazers and jackets can be tricky. They don't hang as well and aren't as comfortable.

Style parameters: stay with a moderate lapel width, not too skinny, not to wide. If you can, select a blazer with double vents in back, rather than the single vent that's more common. This will allow the blazer to still hang well if you put a hand in your pants pocket. Gold or silver blazer buttons are standard equipment. The single-breasted model will serve you better than the double-breasted as it looks just as good with dress or casual pants. Buy the model with the flap (hidden) pockets and not the patch (visible) pockets.

Best uses: most appropriate for dressy to elegant occasions, including a bump up in 'business casual' settings, weddings, elegant dinners, parent-teacher meetings, interviewing for that important internship, sporting events (as a spectator), cocktails with significant others, and yukking it up on someone else's yacht. A little casual for funerals, but if it's all you've got, wear a black necktie, white shirt, and grey slacks. You'll be fine, or at least forgiven.

Usually worn with: grey or tan slacks, chinos, cotton pants, jeans.

Never worn with: suit pants. Only the suit jacket is worn with the suit pants.

Acceptable options: if you've just received a hefty year-end bonus from your Wall Street investment firm and feel compelled to attend those ever-so-delightful Hamptons polo matches in style, take the nonstop to London, visit Turnbull and Asser, and acquire their double-breasted classic blue blazer for twelve hundred bucks or so. And don't mind all those beautiful shirt fabrics on the shelves. We'll get to those later.

If you only buy one: buy the single-breasted, two-button, double-vent model.

Preferred vendors: O'Connell's Clothing of Buffalo, NY, Brooks Brothers, Ralph Lauren. Off the rack with minor alterations. If you decide to upgrade to made-to-measure or bespoke at a later date, start with WW Chan in Hong Kong, then upward to Mariano Rubinacci in Naples, Italy, or Anderson and Sheppard in London.

How to care for it: dry clean only.

Approximate price points: $300.00 to $1200.00 for Off The Rack.

Things to remember: when you try on any jacket, wear a long sleeve dress shirt. This will give you a real feel for how the jacket will wear, and offer you the best chance to select the right size.

You should let your arms hang straight down. As you do, you should just be able to cup your fingers under the tail of the jacket. If you can do that, you have a jacket that's the correct length.

If you can't cup your fingers under the tail, the jacket is too long. If your palms extend below the tail, or the jacket sleeves are the same length as the tail, the jacket is too short.

You should also be able to comfortably button the jacket without the fabric stretching around your waist area. The jacket collar should fit snug against your shirt collar with the jacket buttoned. If it lifts back and away from the shirt collar, the jacket is too small.

Also make sure that the blazer is cut in the classic style: long enough in the tail to cover your butt, short enough in the sleeve to see a quarter inch of shirt cuff fabric, with enough room in the shoulder for a sweater to be worn underneath, but not too much room as to appear baggy.

Things to avoid: clever or novelty linings inside the blazer, garish buttons, top-stitching on the lapels or buttonholes in a contrasting color.

THE TWEED JACKET

Description: this garment is a 100% wool jacket with a full lining. It is a cold-weather garment meant to handle the chill and rain with no small measure of panache.

History, if you care: invented out of necessity by our brothers in Scotland and Ireland who needed to keep warm and dry, the fabric was originally handwoven and incredibly rough.

As the outdoors became a 'thing to do' in the mid 1800s, having the appropriate clothes to do it in became a necessity for British men.

Hence, the rough but incredibly warm tweed fabric surged into the marketplace. Some of the designs initially leaned toward the three-quarter length tweed hunting coat, but more often than not it was the tweed jacket that became the preferred garment to wear while exploring the Scottish Highlands or fly fishing in a misty stream.

While manufacturing processes have made the fabric and garment easier to weave and produce, the style, construction, and fabric of the tweed jacket really haven't changed much in over 100 years. It's still versatile and still elegant today, a good sign of a good investment.

Common colors & fabrics: 100% rough-finished wool that is usually earth-tone in color with some subtle checks in it. Harris Tweed and Donegal tweed are solid options.

Construction details: may have patch (visible) pockets, a more casual option, but most of the time resembles any other jacket with flap (hidden) pockets. It's warmer than the blue blazer and can withstand some moisture.

Note: the heavier the jacket in weight, the more warmth and protection you'll have when you wear it.

Style parameters: again, stay with the soft, natural shoulders, and the same sizing guidelines we discussed with the blue blazer, i.e., double vents and two-button. Well made models will have working button holes on the sleeves, a nice touch.

Best uses: this jacket is best in the fall or winter. Perfect for a walk in the country or visiting museums in the city. A little more casual than the blue blazer, not quite as appropriate for 'business'. Great for travel.

Usually worn with: wool slacks or corduroys, sometimes khakis or jeans, sweaters, dress shoes or boots. You can wear a tie with this jacket.

Never worn with: linen pants.

Acceptable options: the Brits still make 3 button models of these, as it buttons up higher on the torso and keeps you warmer. Feel free.

I wouldn't recommend going made-to-measure or bespoke with the tweed jacket. It communicates such a functional, no-nonsense vibe that, to me, it's counter-in-tuitive to have it fit absolutely perfectly. Especially since you'll probably wear a sweater underneath half the time.

If you only buy one: the single-breasted herringbone brown overcheck model made by Harris Tweed Isle of Harris.

Preferred vendors: Harris Tweed, J Press, Brooks Brothers, O'Connell's. Off the rack with minor alterations.

How to care for it: dry clean only.

Approximate price points: $250 to $750.00.

Things to remember: the single-breasted, two-button, double-vent tweed jacket is a versatile, even elegant mainstay. Great for chilly weather and social but physical outings (translation: pub crawls). When you try one on and consider purchasing it, remember to leave yourself enough room in the shoulders to wear a sweater underneath.

Things to avoid: the black or grey tweed jacket.

The Business Suit

Description: this is a jacket and pants (and perhaps vest) ensemble in which the fabric, color, and style of the jacket is identical to the pants. The jacket and pants were made to be worn together and are always worn together.

History, if you care: suits have been the traditional attire worn by men when conducting business, practicing government, and attending important events like christenings, graduations, weddings, and funerals. You'd think they'd been around forever, but that's not the case.

The start of the 1800s still found men in knee breeches, tails, and powdered wigs. Englishman Beau Brummell changed all that. An Eton graduate and Oxford dropout, he discarded the common wardrobe affectations of the day—impractical, puffy, and bejeweled ensembles worn by the nobility and merchant class—and fashioned himself a tailored and supremely wearable suit of clothes that a man could actually walk and work in.

Obviously, the style of the man's business suit has changed over the decades since then. Lapels, coat lengths, and trouser widths have morphed and contoured. But the concept of a unified, sober, yet elegant ensemble remains.

The two-piece or three-piece business suits of the late 1930s are not that different from suits worn today. In the last ten to fifteen years, suits have been worn less in business settings. Still, it's good to own at least one.

Common colors & fabrics: solid navy blue, grey, and sometimes black are the primary colors and safest options to start with. The fabric is 100% wool and varies in weight. Some suit fabrics are good for year 'round wear (best option). Some fabrics are better for winter, and some fabrics are better for spring and summer. For our purposes, all suit options are wool. No shiny finishes, please.

Construction details: this garment's exterior will be wool, with a silk-like lining inside the jacket. Shoulders will have some padding. Four buttons on the jacket cuffs. Working jacket cuff button holes are a plus. Pants will probably not have a hem. This will be measured and sewn when you purchase or when you take them to your tailor. Expect to have a tailor alter the waist size as well.

Style parameters: go with the natural shoulder, traditional length, double, single, or no vent option, two-button single breasted. Plain front pants with cuffs are preferable.

Best uses: if you work in law, finance, government, high-end sales, or the corporate world, you will probably wear a suit to work regularly. Suits are appropriate for weddings, funerals, church services, elegant evenings out, and important meetings.

Usually worn with: a long sleeve dress shirt and tie. *Please wear a tie with your suit.* So few men know how to wear a suit without a tie, and it's fatiguing to constantly be exposed to the misfires. Set an example. Make the effort. If you want to skip the necktie, fall back to the blazer or jacket with slacks.

Never worn with: a short sleeve shirt, a polo shirt, or a T-shirt.

Acceptable options: it's possible to wear a high quality, thin weave cotton or cashmere sweater underneath your suit jacket. It provides warmth, but makes the look less formal. After you have your blue, grey, or black suit working for you, you may move into a tan, a brown, a pinstripe or a check, but keep the patterns subdued, and stay predominantly with blue and grey as you expand your roster.

When you run the company or have sold the company, feel free to investigate tasteful made-to-measure or bespoke suit options. WW Chan in Hong Kong is a good starting point for about $2000.00 per suit, with a classic British-influenced style that will look good for years. Plan at least 7 days in the city, eat great food, and lose some money at the casinos in neighboring Macau while they cut and construct your garments.

Anderson and Sheppard in London and Mariano Rubinacci in Napoli are the places men with resources go before they die to experience paradise on earth. Enjoy the experience of having suits made for you, and only you, but have your personal banker on speed dial for the wire transfers, because the zeros are going to fly. And don't be in a hurry. The bespoke process requires several fittings and no small amount of thought. Enjoy the ride.

If you only buy one: buy the solid color navy blue suit.

Preferred vendors: Brooks Brothers, Ralph Lauren, J Press. O'Connell's of Buffalo, NY. Off the rack with minor alterations.

(Again, I don't receive any compensation from the vendors I recommend. They just have a track record for quality and customer service.)

How to care for it: dry clean only.

Approximate price points: $950.00 to as much as you want to spend. Watch for sales and discounts if you're not wearing a suit every week.

Things to remember: weigh the amount of money you're going to spend on a suit against the number of times you're going to wear it in a given year. If you're like most men, you'll end up in a blue blazer or jacket more often than not. So calculate your investment accordingly.

Wear only black or brown dress shoes with a suit. Wear only navy blue, chocolate brown, or black socks with a suit.

Button only the top button of a two-button suit jacket, blazer, or jacket.

Things to avoid: suit styles that are too short and too tight. You should have a measure of comfort in the shoulders and be able to button the jacket with ease. The pants should button at your natural waist (your navel) and not on your hips (like jeans often do). The suit pants should not be cut tight and low like jeans or casual pants. The cuffs of your suit pants should just touch your shoes.

THE SUMMER SUIT

Description: a more casual spring and summer suit, to be worn ideally between Easter and the end of August.

History, if you care: seersucker fabric was originally worn by the working class who needed something comfortable to wear in hot weather. College students in the 1920s co-opted the functional and comfortable fabric and made it their own.

One of the offspring of this phenomenon was the seersucker suit, which soon became a spring and summer favorite of well dressed men.

The khaki suit, like all things khaki, has its origins in the British military. The comfort, durability, and classic color soon found their way from the commander's office to the corner office, but, again, only in spring and summer.

Despite the more casual tone that these suits convey with their lighter colors and cooler, lightweight fabrics, they retain an odd formality: you just don't see men wearing them without a tie. It just doesn't look right, and most men seem to instinctively know that.

Today, it's the single-breasted, two-button models that remain most popular for both the seersucker and khaki suit. Elegant options in the age of global warming.

Common colors & fabrics: seersucker, usually in light blue and white stripes, or the khaki in eggshell or the darker, British shade.

Construction details: sometimes half-lined or unlined for comfort. One of the few suits you can go with that way and have it still look good.

Style parameters: usual jacket rules apply. The single-breasted models on this jacket are preferred. They're cooler.

Best uses: this suit is great for summer weddings, elegant beach parties, networking for that internship on capitol hill, and looking good anytime the temperatures climb.

Usually worn with: white dress shirt with the seersucker. Oxford cloth button down blue dress shirt with the khaki. And a mint julep in hand with either.

Never worn with: black shoes.

Acceptable options: the linen suit is an elegant but high-maintenance choice.

If you only buy one: the blue and white seersucker suit.

Preferred vendors: Brooks Brothers.

How to care for it: dry clean only.

Approximate price points: $250.00 to $750.00.

Things to remember: this is a really casual suit. This is not an essential suit.

Things to avoid: pink seersucker. It's just too much.

THE LINEN JACKET

Description: a more casual spring and summer garment, to be worn ideally between Easter and the end of August. (In Los Angeles and Miami, it's open season for you guys.)

History, if you care: in the late 1800s, suit fabric was almost universally made of dark and heavy wool. Only the very rich could afford to keep a light-colored garment clean, and so anything made of lighter, brighter linen was the mark of an affluent gentleman.

In the 1930s, advertisements began to promote double-breasted linen jackets as a mainstream alternative for leisure and office wear. Palm Beach, Florida, became the epicenter of the linen jacket, worn with pride by the trendy and the tanned.

Men's fashion sobered up during World War II and immediately thereafter. Linen garments fell out of fashion for awhile. Only in the early 1980s did linen come back on the radar.

With today's more relaxed dress standards for both the workplace and social events, linen jackets are back in favor. Current styles have been perfected by the Neapolitans, where the southern Italian summers are absolutely sweltering, but the men are genetically hard-wired to look good year 'round. Not a critical garment to own, but a nice option to have.

Common colors & fabrics: 100% linen, a wheat color is usually best, but blue is also great.

Construction details: one of the few jackets that is often unlined for comfortable wear in warmer climates. Never has shoulder padding. A bit more fitted than a normal jacket, and may be just a little shorter in the tail to be more casual.

Style parameters: usual jacket rules apply, although the lapels may be narrower on this jacket and still look okay.

Best uses: this jacket is great for summer weddings, elegant beach parties, Sunday brunch with family and friends, and looking good anytime the temperatures climb.

Usually worn with: white cotton dress shirt, linen pants, cotton pants, jeans, casual shoes.

Never worn with: wool pants, khakis, black shoes.

Acceptable options: you'll see a double-breasted model every once in a while. If you're slim, give it a shot.

If you only buy one: go with the single-breasted, wheat or eggshell-colored model.

Preferred vendors: You'll find good-looking models made by a variety of designers. Pick a good fabric weight, not too thin. Off the rack with minor alterations.

How to care for it: dry clean only.

Approximate price points: $250.00 to $750.00.

Things to remember: this is a really casual jacket. This is an optional jacket.

Things to avoid: looking like a Miami Vice throwback.

The Tuxedo

Description: a black formal jacket with black pants, black bow tie, black vest or cummerbund, worn with black patent leather shoes or black velvet slippers. Worn for events designated as 'formal' or 'black tie'. Almost always evening wear.

History, if you care: most accurately referred to as 'the dinner jacket', the tuxedo gets its name from its early usage in Tuxedo Park, New York, more than a century ago.

But, again, we have to give a begrudging nod to sartorial brothers across the pond: Prince Edward, weary of wearing the very formal tailcoat everywhere, sent tongues wagging with his scandalous move into the dinner jacket in 1865.

It wasn't as formal as tails, but more formal than what was then known as a 'lounge suit'. How the dinner jacket made its way from England to America is unknown. The name 'tuxedo', as we mentioned, refers to Tuxedo Park, an affluent community in New York state. It was here that wealthy industrialists of the era dressed in their dinner jackets, or 'tuxedos', for dinner.

In the 1940s, business suits became the preferred attire for elegant evenings out. Tuxedos were relegated to 'formal events' like awards shows, charity galas, and diplomatic receptions.

Today, tuxedos are seldom worn, and seldom worn well, but we'll do our best to correct that.

The good news is that, like so many of our Old Money Style garments, the tuxedo hasn't really changed in concept, construction, or design in almost 100 years. A comforting thought.

Common colors & fabrics: The tuxedo, my good man, is always black, and always wool.

Construction details: The body of the suit and pants is wool. The lapels of the suit are satin, with a shiny finish. There is a satin strip that runs down the outside seam of the pants leg.

The cummerbund is a pleated satin waist garment that encircles the torso and covers the area between the tuxedo shirt and the tuxedo pants. The second option is the vest, which is usually wool but can be satin. Like the cummerbund, both are always black. Vest or cummerbund, please. One or the other. Required.

Style parameters: a tuxedo can be single-breasted or double-breasted, but the lapel on a proper tuxedo is always a shawl collar or peaked lapel collar, never a notched collar. If you care about this kind of thing—and you should—research it online. Learn the appropriate style parameters of formal attire. These will serve you well.

A tuxedo shirt is always worn with the tuxedo. The tuxedo shirt is white. Styles of collar, cuffs, and pleats vary on tuxedo shirts, but do not include ruffles. Only a black bowtie is worn with a tuxedo. Unless you are the star of an action film, always wear a bowtie with a tuxedo. Do not wear a necktie with a tuxedo.

If you encounter someone with a differing opinion on these critical formalwear issues, smile politely, change the subject, and reconsider your friendship with them. (And don't allow anyone to site examples of celebrities in tuxedos on the red carpet as proof of anything. Celebrities are frequently incredibly wrong when it comes to clothes, and especially tuxedos.)

Best uses: sometimes required for holiday parties, big-time celebrations, movie premieres, and gala fundraisers. Invitations to these events should include the directive 'black tie' or 'formal'. If the invitation says 'formal', make sure the hosts mean 'black tie' and not just 'dark suit, white shirt, dark tie.' Ask. And never just 'decide' to wear a tuxedo to an event. You may be alone in your decision and perhaps mistaken for a waiter.

Usually worn with: black patent leather shoes or black velvet slippers. By 'slippers' I do not mean house shoes that you wear with pajamas. There are men's velvet slippers that you can purchase. They are perfect with a tux, but also look great with a pair of faded jeans and, yes, a tuxedo shirt unbuttoned at the collar. The ensemble is sophisticated, stylish, dashing, and totally contrary to everything else I'm advocating. But don't tell anyone.

Never worn with: a plain white dress shirt.

Acceptable options: The rare Plan B is the white dinner jacket worn for special events in tropical climates. (See Humphrey Bogart in *Casablanca* who, by the way, is appropriately and perfectly outfitted in a white shawl collar tuxedo jacket and a black peaked-lapel dinner jacket).

Another elegant option is the velvet smoking jacket in black or the lovely midnight blue. Most appropriate when you're entertaining the friends at home with a private, catered dinner that will be followed by a high-stakes game of pool (billiards) and ample amount of bubbly. Again, best to see Anderson and Sheppard for this one.

If you only buy one: Don't buy it at all, to start with anyway. If you are wearing a tuxedo once or twice a year, rent it. Buy a high quality tuxedo shirt and a well-made pair of formal shoes. Own those, and sandwich the rented tuxedo in between them to start. Don't invest in this garment unless you wear one three or four times a year. Only then is it worth it. And, unless you're really living some kind of life, you only need one.

Preferred vendors: for tuxedos, Ralph Lauren, Brooks Brothers. For velvet slippers, Crockett and Jones, Smythe and Digby, Brooks Brothers.

How to care for it: dry clean only for the tux. Soft brush for the slippers.

Approximate price points: $1750.00 to $3500.00 for the tux. $150.00 to $500.00 for the slippers.

Things to remember: tuxedos were created so that all the men at an event would look the same and blend into the background. This would allow the women at the event to sparkle, and to be the center of everyone's attention. So keep it black, keep it clean, keep it simple.

Things to avoid: anything not black. Tuxedo shirts that are not white.

THE SHIRTS

The Dress Shirt

Description: the dress shirt is the garment that covers your torso and arms when you get dressed. You wear it with pants, sweaters, jackets, blazers, and suits, the most durable and most versatile option being the light blue oxford cloth button down (OCBD) with long sleeves and button cuffs.

The dress shirt can be worn every day. It is omnipresent, given the fact that the shirt may be the first and main thing people notice about your wardrobe. It should be a priority when you look at upgrading your wardrobe. Personally, I have a passion for great dress shirts. For these two reasons, I'll spend a little more time on the dress shirt than other garments.

History, if you care: up until the 1800s, men's shirts were a primitive, one-size-fits-all affair with huge sleeves, billowing torsos, drawstrings at the cuffs and collar, and not much in the way of color (all white).

Charvet, the legendary French shirtmaker, changed all that, giving some method to the madness, some form to the function, some structure to the garment.

Until Charvet was founded in the 1830s, men who wanted a shirt bought the fabric themselves and took it to a cutter (usually a linen merchant). The cutter then sliced the fabric into primitive shapes, sewed the bulky pieces of cloth together, and called it a day.

Christophe Charvet acquired his own fabric and measured his clients in his Paris shop. He constructed and defined the collar, sleeve, and cuff, and tapered the body of the shirt. The son of Napoleon's wardrobe master, his clientele began as a small circle of well-heeled Parisians. But his innovations to the dress shirt's style, form, and function still resonate around the world, almost 200 years later.

Today, the dress shirt most men wear hasn't changed much at all in the last 100 years. They still button up the front. The cuffs on long sleeve shirts have buttons. They're designed to be tucked inside the pants.

Collar styles expand and contract, spread and narrow, slowly, back and forth over decades. But if you look at a photo of a well-dressed man from the 1940s—say,

Gary Cooper or Cary Grant—their shirts would, for the most part, look good today.

Common colors & fabrics: The dress shirt is always 100% cotton, best in white, light blue, or what's called a 'bengal' or 'university' stripe, in blue and white. Oxford cloth is a sturdy go-to fabric and a good place to start. Broadcloth, Egyptian cotton, and other softer, thinner, but less durable fabrics are also available.

Construction details: The dress shirt buttons all the way up the front and can button at the top to accommodate a necktie. The thicker, mother of pearl buttons are a sign of a well-made shirt.

It is best if the same fabric, color, and pattern are used for the entire shirt. If you develop an interest in dress shirts, you will come to appreciate the variety of fabrics that are available, and how they can serve you in terms of comfort, style, and durability.

The dress shirt usually has single buttons on the cuff, and may have what's called a 'double cuff' or 'French cuff', which requires cuff links. The collar folds down, away from the face. It may or may not have a front breast pocket. (Best not.)

Style parameters: The most reliable shirt collars are the traditional spread collar and the button down collar. They work with most jackets, suits, and sweaters, look good with or without a necktie.

The traditional spread collar is just a normal shirt collar you see all the time. The collar points descend from the neck down toward the chest at about a 45 degree angle. Sometimes more, sometimes less.

The button down collar is not quite as formal, but still works with everything— jackets, blazers, and suits—just fine. The button or barrel cuffs are more practical and versatile than the French cuffs. The button cuffs can be worn with any garment, and work really well under sweaters.

The French or double cuff is a more formal shirt, usually worn with a suit. Cufflinks hold the cuff together. Please keep your cufflinks simple and small, gold or silver, subtle and refined. Avoid the clever or the political.

Upscale men's clothing stores will offer 'silk knot' cufflinks which are small woven silk knots, as the name implies, that are pushed through the cuff holes to keep the cuffs in place. These come in a variety of colors and are an elegant alternative to a metallic cufflink.

Best uses: You can wear a dress shirt all the time, everywhere, so It's best to buy a shirt than you can wear dress or casual, winter, spring, summer or fall. So keep it to a blue or white, a solid or a stripe, long sleeve, with a more durable fabric.

Usually worn with: everything.

Never worn with: scuba gear.

Acceptable options: the cutaway collar with French cuffs can work, if you know how to wear it and what it communicates. Collar and cuffs in white fabric with a different color or striped torso and sleeve is another, bolder option. Like the cutaway collar, the contrast communicates a slightly more rebellious attitude. (See Gordon Gekko in the movie 'Wall Street'.)

Note: the 'contrasting collar' style doesn't look good unless the shirt is really, really well-made, preferably made-to-measure or bespoke. The rest of your ensemble— the jacket, pants or suit, and shoes—must be top-shelf, too, or you look like you spent all your money on your shirt, which is lame. People can tell. So know before you go.

If you've just made partner at the firm or just closed that big transaction, grab your passport. Again, it's all aboard to Turnbull and Asser in London and for a review of their colorful collection of shirting fabrics. Don't forget the equally-colorful ties, and ask yourself how they'd look with those conservative suits you wear. The answer: smashing.

Then, take a first class seat on the Eurostar from London San Pancras to Gare du Nord in Paris. Check into the Ritz. Saunter confidently across the Place Vendome to Charvet, where over 5,000 shirting fabrics await your consideration, including over 400 varieties in white alone. (A famous client of Charvet once remarked that this was the place that the rainbow came to get ideas for colors.)

Enter the high temple of shirts. Stroll the ground floor showroom with over 1,000 neckties on display. Consider Charvet's fine ready-made shirts. Ponder bespoke collar and cuff options (20 or 30 choices of each). Ask to see the upstairs fabric room, where rows and rows of the finest cotton weaves known to man await your review, stacked from floor to ceiling, wall to wall. Climb the stairs. Breathe in the history. Feel the fabrics. Consider the possibilities.

Finally, take a quick flight down to Napoli and consult with the lovely ladies at Anna Matuozzo's hidden gem of an atelier, where you can have bespoke shirts constructed in the finest Neapolitan tradition. Marvel at the exuberant collars and snug cuffs, the torso tailored to embrace and define.

Walk the narrow streets. Banter with street vendors. Pray for guidance inside any one of the many magnificent cathedrals in Naples. Enjoy some of the finest cuisine Italy has to offer: the calamari, the capellini pomodoro, the limoncello. Contemplate your shirting options as you enjoy a coffee and a 'rhum baba' at the legendary Cafe Gambrinus. Know that life is good.

If you only buy one: the iconic oxford cloth button down in light blue from Mercer and Sons Shirts.

Preferred vendors: Mercer and Sons, Ralph Lauren, Brooks Brothers, LL Bean. Off the rack until you have the need/desire/budget to move into made-to-measure or bespoke. Then it's Charvet, Turnbull & Asser, and Anna Matuozzo.

How to care for it: cold water wash, let your shirts hang dry. If you machine dry, expect accelerated wear and possible shrinkage. Warm or hot iron. Wooden hangers. And don't play rugby in your dress shirts.

Stain remover applied pre-wash to the collars and cuffs if you perspire heavily. Just a *tiny* bit of bleach every once in awhile to bounce up the white dress shirts in your rotation.

Approximate price points: $75.00 to $200.00 (for Turnbull and Asser, Charvet, and Anna Matuozzo, made-to-measure and bespoke options will start at 350 euros and go up from there.)

Things to remember: if you've got a classic blue blazer and a 3 or 4 quality dress shirts, you're half-way there in terms of having a solid wardrobe.

Over time, the collar and cuffs on a dress shirt may fray from wear. If the shirt is good quality, and especially if it's made-to-measure or bespoke, these can be replaced by the shirtmaker, extending the life of the shirt.

Your shirt and your shoes will tell on you, so invest in quality with both.

Things to avoid: short sleeve dress shirts.

THE POLO SHIRT

Description: the polo shirt is a pullover 100% cotton short sleeve shirt with a short collar and 3-button front, buttoning from the breastbone up to the neck.

History, if you care: the style was originally worn by polo players in the 1920s. The original models had buttons to hold the collars down; the polo players didn't like the collars flipping up and slapping them in the face as they rode on horseback at full speed during matches.

At about the same time, French tennis legend Rene Lacoste introduced his version, and then launched his namesake company in 1933 with the crocodile logo. The Lacoste polo has been a legendary product since its introduction and is a favorite among European men.

In 1972, Ralph Lauren introduced his version of the pullover 3-button cotton shirt. It has been his best-selling product for the last 50 years.

Common colors & fabrics: comes in a variety of solid colors, stripes, and a wide variety of natural and synthetic fabrics. We should all stay with solids and 100% cotton.

Construction details: made for active and even athletic use and abuse (touch football, being the 'horse' your four-year old rides on). The best fabric has a rough finish and wears like iron. Opt for the models with elastic bands on the sleeves to give you arms definition. The Ralph Lauren model has a longer shirt tale in the back of the shirt than in the front. This prevents it from becoming untucked from your pants as easily.

Style parameters: pop the collar up if you want to get your full prep effect going, or if, like me, your neck gets cold. Don't wear the polo shirt baggy. It looks awful in a size too large. Comes in a slim fit, which is preferable for gents with a lean figure.

Best uses: golf, tennis, the beach, camping, college, road trips. Great when you don't feel like ironing a shirt, or if you think a nap on the sofa might be in the forecast at some point later that day.

Usually worn with: cotton pants, khakis, jeans, shorts, underneath sweaters or underneath button down dress shirts. For the full-prep look, throw on the polo, then a button down, then a sweater, then a tweed jacket.

Never worn with: wool dress pants, suits, blazers, or jackets, unless you have just won the Masters golf tournament.

Acceptable options: the rugby shirt is a long sleeve option of similar construction that also works for casual occasions.

If you only buy one: the navy blue Ralph Lauren polo shirt.

Preferred vendors: Ralph Lauren, Lacoste, Brooks Brothers.

How to care for it: cold water wash, cool tumble dry it if you like. Expect a little shrinkage if you tumble dry hot, but it also gives it a nice, worn look over time.

Approximate price points: $60.00 to $120.00

Things to remember: dark colors will work best for you over time as they're less likely to show stains and look better as they age.

Things to avoid: logos that are more than one inch tall.

The T-Shirt

Description: a white or grey cotton pullover shirt with no collar that is worn underneath another shirt.

History, if you care: originally part of a one-piece men's undergarment, the T-shirt broke away from the underpants as miners, working in unbelievable hot conditions, wore them as a comfortable alternative to shirts in the late 1800s. During the Great Depression, they became acceptable for the lads working on farms and ranches. The 1950s saw T-shirts become accepted as casual clothing, and in the 1960s wearing a T-shirt with something printed on it became an all-too-common phenomenon.

Common colors & fabrics: white is the most common color, always 100% cotton.

Construction details: usually has a reinforced collar and sometimes reinforced tale. Short sleeves are usually not ribbed.

Style parameters: not much to say here, as T-shirts are pretty uniform in construction and style.

Best uses: I hate to break this to you, dear reader, but a T-shirt is underwear. It is not a garment that qualifies as 'casual attire'. In polite society, it is worn underneath a dress shirt to keep you warm, or to keep sweat off of your dress shirt. If exposed to the public, it is best worn only while exercising, on the basketball court, or lifting weights.

When you're finished exercising, the sooner you can put on a sweatshirt or warm-up top, the better for everyone. Yes, I know this sounds Old School and pissy, but it's just not a good look, regardless of how physically fit you are.

Worst uses: if worn while doing a Ted Talk.

Usually worn with: jeans and athletic shoes, sadly. With a sport coat, horribly. The white T-shirt is best worn under a blue oxford cloth button down dress shirt. Clean and classic.

Never worn with: I honestly wish I could think of something that I haven't seen a T-shirt worn with.

Acceptable options: on this one, could we say 'a better option'? That would be the polo shirt.

If you only buy one: a white T-shirt that you wear under another shirt.

Preferred vendors: Hanes. For the best T-shirts (and underwear) in the world, visit a Zimmerli boutique.

How to care for it: machine wash, cool tumble dry.

Approximate price points: $10.00 to $30.00.

Things to remember: keep T-shirts pristine white, functional, and hidden. Wearing a T-shirt in public doesn't present your best image. Upgrade with a little effort to Old Money Style.

Things to avoid: T-shirts with things written on them. When you wear a T-shirt with something written on it, you're handing over all of your personal power to that brand, message, or logo. You have purchased the T-shirt and paid good money for the privilege of advertising someone else's brand for them.

If you're going to promote a brand, promote your own brand: yourself.

THE SWEATER

Description: the sweater is a woven cotton, wool, and sometimes cashmere garment that is usually worn over a shirt.

History, if you care: knitting wool by hand has been around for about 2000 years. In the late 1400s, the wives of fisherman in the British Isles wove some heavy-duty models for their husbands to protect them from the chilling mist of the English Channel and its biting cold.

Innovations and inventions in the textile industry—like the power loom in 1785—made the sweater a mass-produced item, marketed and sold the world over. In the 1890s, American athletes adopted a navy blue crew-neck style, and the name 'sweater' was born.

Today, sweaters still perform their primary function—to keep us warm. Accommodating function and fashion, zippers and buttons have been added, but the same crew-neck, V-neck, cardigan, and turtleneck styles remain.

Common colors & fabrics: best when they're 100% wool or 100% cotton. The wool versions look great in a light grey or wheat, but can also work really well in navy blue, dark green, and burgundy.

Cotton sweaters in navy blue are standard equipment. It's acceptable to enjoy lighter shades of blue and pastels, especially in the crew-neck models, and especially when you drift toward warmer climates.

Construction details: can be cable knit, with a rough (fuzzy) or smooth finish. The quality of the sweater lies in the tightness of the weave and the sturdiness of the construction around the neck and cuffs.

Style parameters: the classic options are the V-neck, crew-neck, cardigan, and roll neck, often referred to as a turtleneck. The crew-neck is the go-to model.

The roll neck is the only sweater that you can wear without a shirt underneath.

Best uses: the sweater is the first layer you throw on, over your dress shirt or your polo shirt, when the weather turns cold. It's casual, comfortable, functional. Best to keep it in solid colors and be cool with the cable knit.

Usually worn with: dress shirts, polo shirts, tweed jackets, casual pants, dress pants. Can go with a blazer. Rarely will you wear a sweater with a suit, but some guys can pull it off.

Never worn with: if it's a wool sweater, you wouldn't wear it with linen pants.

Acceptable options: tennis sweaters, argyle sweaters. (Enjoy the movie 'Caddyshack' for a sweater feast.)

If you only buy one: the navy blue crew-neck, in wool or cotton. If money is no object, the Shaggy Dog sweater from J. Press in dove grey.

Preferred vendors: J. Press, Ralph Lauren, Brooks Brothers, LL Bean, Lands' End. Consider Loro Piana at the top end.

How to care for it: dry clean or hand wash the cotton sweater; dry clean the wool ones.

Approximate price points: $60.00 to $300.00.

Things to remember: make sure your sweaters fit. Baggy sweaters don't give you the best look, especially if you're slim. Try it on in the store, over a dress shirt, before you buy. Make sure the shoulder seams rest on your shoulder bone, not your arm, and be aware of how much loose fabric you have in the torso.

Part of Old Money Style is layering. Feel free to wear a layered combination of polo shirt, dress shirt, sweater, and tweed jacket when the weather dictates.

Things to avoid: Christmas sweaters. Vest sweaters. Sweaters obviously from the 1980s.

THE VEST

Description: the vest is a sleeveless garment that buttons up the front, from just below the waistline to the breastbone. It is most appropriately and commonly worn under a jacket or as the third part of a three-piece suit.

History, if you care: thought to have originally come from Persia, where the temperatures are warm and men don't always need a full jacket, the vest was then reincarnated in France. In the mid 1600s, French monarch Charles II wanted a way to differentiate himself from his court, so he went all floral and embroidered with his vest, and made it official with a royal decree, as if that was necessary.

The vest, or waistcoat as its known in the UK, continued to be a part of the well-dressed man's wardrobe throughout the following centuries. In the 1800s the vest became an essential part of a man's suit. You wouldn't go out in public without one.

Dandies—men overly concerned with looking stylish or fashionable—of the 20th century donned vests in every color and fabric imaginable, pairing it with the business suit, as well as the jacket and slacks. But the idea that your suit had to have a vest was long gone by the 1950s.

Today the vest is most often worn as an extra layer of warmth and an extra touch of style, as a personal choice. No royal decree required.

Common colors & fabrics: 100% wool is the most common and appropriate fabric for the front, with a silk or satin fabric for the back and interior of the garment. Best in earth tones or small, muted checks.

Construction details: most vests do not have lapels, but some dressier models do. 8 to 12 buttons generally run vertically from the top front to the bottom front of the garment. Sometimes there's a small cinch to tighten the torso of the vest in the back and give it a more fitted look on leaner gents.

Style parameters: keep the vest single-breasted with subtle brass, gold, silver, or horn buttons. Avoid the silk or satin models, or vests intended to be worn with a tuxedo.

Best uses: the vest dresses up an ensemble, so if you're going to a casual dinner and you want to dress up the tweed jacket and jeans, put a wool vest on over your dress shirt and under your jacket, and rock it. It might not be as warm as a sweater, but it looks far more elegant.

Usually worn with: a tweed jacket or blazer, wool dress pants, and even jeans. Lace-up shoes look better with a vest than loafers, for some reason. A necktie can add an almost-formal look.

Never worn with: short sleeve shirt, T-shirt, or linen pants.

Acceptable options: the red wool vest is a lively option, especially for parties around Christmas and New Year's. If you're Scottish, of course you'd be eligible to sport a vest showing off your clan's tartan. If you can find a dove grey flannel vest, buy it and wear it with your navy business suit for a snappy look at weddings and elegant soirees.

If you only buy one: a muted houndstooth check in tan, chocolate brown, or forest green.

Preferred vendors: Pendleton, Harris Tweed, Brooks Brothers, and, surprisingly, vintage stores, who seem to have a large collection of wool vests in good condition.

How to care for it: dry clean only, and don't gain weight.

Approximate price points: $60 to $145.00.

Things to remember: leave that bottom button on your vest unbuttoned. It's a style thing when you're standing and a comfort thing when you're sitting.

Things to avoid: sweater vests, unless it's the tennis version and you're playing tennis.

THE PANTS

COTTON PANTS

Description: 100% cotton long pants with a plain front (or pleat).

History, if you care: khakis, the most popular cotton pants, were a 19th century innovation. British soldiers whose wool uniforms were too hot for the sweltering temperatures of India opted for cotton, which was definitely cooler. In 1867, the British army officially adopted khaki for their uniforms, and in 1898, the U.S. army followed suit, so to speak.

In the early 20th century, khakis met and quickly fell in love with the blue blazer. For Old Money Guys, it seemed like a match made in heaven.

However, colorful cotton pants in a multitude of tempting shades and patterns were introduced to the men's fashion landscape in the late 1950s. The blue blazer ventured out and began to enjoy the company of other pants, but still remained (somewhat) loyal to khakis.

Today, the khakis still retain the title of First Among Equals. They are seen out and about on the professional and social scene, with and without the blue blazer, as are the colored pants. None of them seems jealous of any of the others, which is quite remarkable.

Common colors & fabrics: always 100% cotton. These can be khakis or chinos, which run from the British tan to an eggshell in color grades. The cotton pant can also be olive green, dark blue, or the legendary Nantucket Reds.

Construction details: zip front, usually. Plain front is preferable. Pleats are acceptable. The presence of belt loops is common. May have flaps and buttons on the back pocket to keep your wallet in its place.

Style parameters: as with all garments Old Money, not too tight, not too loose. The better these fit, the better they look. Nothing too gathered around the ankles, no bell bottoms. Asking your tailor to install cuffs on the cotton pants will make them dressier, if you often wear them with a blazer, jacket, and tie. A crisp crease from a serious iron and starch will give you a sharp look for important events.

Best uses: 'business casual' workplace environments, backyard barbecues, ball games, birthday parties. Anything where jeans might be too casual and slacks are a little too dressy. Spring, summer, and fall. Could be a little breezy in the winter, but there's no hard-and-fast rule on the seasons in which you can wear these.

Usually worn with: the dress shirt. The polo shirt. The blue blazer and dress shirt. The tweed jacket and dress shirt. The dress shirt and sweater. Dress shoes or casual shoes.

Never worn with: black lace-up dress shoes.

Acceptable options: go crazy with bright or burnt orange, lime or forest green, teal or French blue, fire engine red, or banana yellow cotton pants. Pair these with a white dress shirt and blue blazer. Ideal for tailgating before the big game, vintage automobile auctions, and dinner with the future in-laws.

If you only buy one: Brooks Brothers 'Clark' model khakis.

Preferred vendors: O'Connell's Clothing, Brooks Brothers, Ralph Lauren, Bill's Khakis, LL Bean, Lands' End.

How to care for it: dry clean if you want that crisp crease look. Machine wash according to label instructions, cool dry or hang dry otherwise. Iron as needed.

Approximate price points: $60.00 to $175.00.

Things to remember: denim jeans can be hot during the summer. Cotton pants can be cooler, and look better.

Things to avoid: madras. Unless you really, truly do not give a damn.

DRESS PANTS

Description: 100% wool slacks cover the lower part of your body, from your waist to your ankles. These are the go-to option for dressier ensembles.

History, if you care: dress pants for men were a knee-length affair until the French revolution, circa 1789, when the citizens of Paris decided to wear their pants down to their ankles, announcing their democratic leanings to one and all.

Pants have pretty much stayed long since then. Rare exceptions might include a gent donning the tweed plus fours (pants that extend just 4 inches below the knee) on the occasional shooting expedition in the British countryside, or the same knee-length, retro fashion on the golf course, complete with colorful argyle socks and two-toned golf shoes.

Contemporary dress pants are now almost always made of wool, a fabric known for its durability and wrinkle resistant nature. Technology over the last 60 years has enabled the wool to be blended in finer weaves, making the fabric more comfortable and more suited for year 'round wear.

Innovations in construction have made the pants versatile, and men's reluctance to buy new pants ever year has forced the fashion industry to change the cut and shape of pants slowly, if at all. That's good news: a quality pair of pants can last years.

Common colors & fabrics: the fundamental garment is the grey, 100% wool, with viable options being tan, chocolate brown, and olive green.

Construction details: most come with belt loops and are not hemmed at the cuff, allowing you to have a tailor measure the length, and giving you the option of cuffs or no cuffs. (cuffs, please.)

Style parameters: plain front and pleats are options. Right now, I'd recommend plain front. Check back with me in ten years. Pleats may make a comeback. Actually, pleats are okay, but can make you look broader across the front.

Best uses: upscale business casual settings, any occasion in which a suit might be too much but khakis or jeans are not enough.

Usually worn with: a blazer or tweed jacket, dress shoes or loafers, for a classic, elegant, but not too formal look.

Never worn with: a polo shirt, suit jacket, or athletic shoes.

Acceptable options: can be worn with only a dress shirt and sweater if you're not feeling the more casual corduroys (discussed later). I wouldn't bother to upgrade to a made-to-measure or bespoke option on dress pants. Quality Off The Rack dress pants with expert alterations can give you the same look for much less money.

If you only buy one: the grey dress slacks in a year 'round wool.

Preferred vendors: O'Connell's Clothing, Brooks Brothers, Ralph Lauren, Lands' End.

How to care for it: dry clean only.

Approximate price points: $60.00 to $200.00.

Things to remember: make sure these aren't too baggy or too long. These can be fitted in the seat and legs and still look good. If they're too long and bunch around the top of your shoes, it looks sloppy. Have your tailor cuff them so they just touch the top of your shoes.

An important part of Old Money Style is covering most of your body with clothes most of the time. Long sleeve shirts. Long pants.

Things to avoid: wearing a linen jacket with 100% wool dress slacks. Don't do it.

Corduroy Pants

Description: Corduroys are a heavier, ribbed finish cotton pant worn in the fall and winter, more casual than the grey wool dress pants.

History, if you care: the fabric looks like it is made from side-by-side 'cords', hence the name…I think. Some historians make reference to the French phrase 'cords du roi' or 'cords of the king', hinting at a royal pedigree for the ribbed cloth. Others point back to ancient Egypt and the creation of a fabric that was *like corduroy*, but didn't have the ribbed cords as a part of it. Which doesn't make any sense to me. Is it corduroy? Or is it something else?

Whatever the origins of the name and the material, the sturdy, often warm, heavier-ribbed fabric was a favorite of the early 20th century working man. Its durability and comfort made it a natural for daily wear in harsh environments.

Trend-wise, it's been hit and miss with corduroys. Most of us missed the 1920s, when super-wide-leg baggy cords were all the rage.

Thankfully, today's cut and style of corduroy pants haven't changed much since the 1950s.

Common colors & fabrics: always 100% cotton, some with a waterproof finish to keep you warm and dry. Colors run the gambit, but chocolate, tan, rust, and dark green will be your starting lineup.

Construction details: corduroys are more often cut like dress pants, with long vertical front pockets on the pants leg seams, than 5 pocket jeans. They are heavier, so you will want belt loops. Your belt will hold them up.

Style parameters: these run from full cut with pleats to tailored. If you are slim, go for the tailored fit, as cords can look baggier than other pants because the fabric is thicker.

Best uses: corduroys are dressy but casual. Not for job interviews or formal occasions like funerals or weddings. Business casual, yes. Holiday cocktail parties, yes. Sporting events, yes. Meeting royalty, no.

Usually worn with: a dress shirt, sweater, and tweed jacket.

Never worn with: a linen blazer.

Acceptable options: like the cotton pants, cords come in a variety of eye-popping colors. Feel free to indulge.

If you only buy one: a chocolate brown pair of high quality cords.

Preferred vendors: O'Connell's Clothing, Ralph Lauren, Brooks Brothers.

How to care for it: dry clean only.

Approximate price points: $60.00 to $175.00

Things to remember: fabric and weave quality can vary widely, and it's difficult to compare without standing in the store, feeling the fabric, and looking at the construction. Take time to do this.

Things to avoid: cheap versions of this garment. They will wear poorly, won't keep you warm, and won't last very long.

Linen Pants

Description: 100% linen pants are an elegant, comfortable, but seasonal option for a man's wardrobe. Not an essential.

History, if you care: originally used to wrap the bodies of pharaohs in ancient Egypt, linen fabric remains a favorite of rich guys in warmer climates who won't be moving very much, very fast, or at all.

From the Roaring '20s up to the present day, the fuller-cut pants have always looked better than any slim fit versions.

The fact that this fabric doesn't wear as well as a wool or (obviously) denim has made linen pants less of a priority when a man thinks of clothing that he really 'needs'. Stay focused on your priorities, and consider these later.

Common colors & fabrics: 100% cotton linen, the natural wheat color is the most popular.

Construction details: cut like dress pants with vertical front pockets and two back pockets. Some are half-lined, to the knee, as linen can be a little revealing (thin). Something to think about as you decide which briefs you're going to wear with which linen pants.

Style parameters: very tailored linen pants kind of defeat the purpose, which is to be cool and comfortable, the man of leisure. The fuller cut allows the fabric to flow as you walk, which looks very elegant. The quality of the linen is the key issue here. Thick in texture, soft to the touch, and rich in color.

Best uses: spring or summer weddings, dining or drinks al fresco, anytime between Easter and the end of summer when looking good trumps wearing something practical. Very, very casual. Do not wear linen pants to any business meeting. Something social, like attending a sporting event with a client, is completely different. Go for it.

Usually worn with: a blue blazer is best. A linen jacket worn with linen pants is a little 'matchy-matchy', but it's okay.

Never worn with: a tweed jacket or wool sweater. Even a cotton sweater with linen pants looks a little funny, but it happens sometimes when the sun sets on some tropical isle.

Acceptable options: the sky blue or tobacco colored linen pant is a nice option with the blue blazer. The bleached white or eggshell linen pant is also nice, but communicates a very 'yacht club' image.

If you only buy one: the wheat color linen pants.

Preferred vendors: with this item, it's more the weight and weave of the linen than any particular vendor.

How to care for it: dry clean.

Approximate price points: $60.00 to $150.00.

Things to remember: you can just look at linen pants and they'll wrinkle. That said, when it's hotter than hell on Sunday, no one will care if you're sporting a lived-in look: you'll be cool and unfazed by the heat in your suave linen pants.

When you are just starting to build your wardrobe, these pants are optional.

Things to avoid: letting your linen pants slip below your waist and ride on your hips. This just looks awful. A well-dressed man knows where his dress pants should fit: at his navel, not below.

DENIM JEANS

Description: the ubiquitous, too-often worn garment that is, admittedly, incredibly durable, versatile, and timeless.

History, if you care: the fabric was originally created in Nimes, France. So when people asked about it, it was referred to as being 'de Nimes' or, 'from Nimes'. This phrase gradually evolved into the word 'denim'.

In the 1870s, Levi Strauss created the first version of the jeans we know today, crafting them for miners during the gold rush in California. The original garments were constructed from canvas. Denim came later.

Since then, hundreds of companies have made millions of denim jeans for billions of people. Profits have undoubtedly soared. Fashion has permanently changed. Standards for appropriate dress have arguably plummeted.

While blue remains the standard for jeans, they are now made in a variety of colors and remain incredibly durable, both in terms of wear and style.

While the convenience and relative economical price tag of denim jeans is difficult to argue, the central issue today seems to be convincing men that jeans are not appropriate attire for all occasions.

Shall we agree to work on this together?

Common colors & fabrics: blue, 100% cotton. Black is also popular, especially in Europe.

Construction details: zip or button fly, plain front, belt loops, 5 pockets.

Style parameters: from baggies to bell bottoms to skinny jeans, designers keep rolling out new models every 5 minutes. Best to go with Levi's 511, 501, or 513. These models are the classics that will look good, and not peg you to a particular decade or trend. Opt for the unfaded and unripped. Time will work its magic on your jeans. No need to rush the process.

Best uses: worn while participating in physical activities like tree removals, rodeos, shooting skeet in West Texas, or shooting the breeze on the Upper West Side. A global option anytime comfort and durability are your primary considerations. Understandable for activities and events that might damage or stain your cotton pants or dress slacks, or when the event is decidedly casual.

Usually worn with: a variety of garments, most of them casual. Not bad with a short sleeve polo shirt.

Never worn with: blue jeans don't really look good with black lace up dress shoes, in my opinion, nor do you wear them with a suit jacket. The black shoes are too formal for the casual nature of jeans. The suit jacket, as you'll remember, is always worn with the matching suit pants.

Acceptable options: it's really best if you dress a pair of jeans up with a dress shirt, tweed jacket or blazer, some loafers or chukka boots, and a very nice brown leather belt.

If you only buy one: Levi's 501 jeans.

Preferred vendors: Levi's.

How to care for it: wash per instructions on the label and dry. Be prepared for a little shrinkage if you dry them with a lot of heat.

Approximate price points: $50.00 to $90.00.

Things to remember: jeans in the workplace are tricky and can give your colleagues the wrong impression, even in today's 'anything goes' professional work environment. Be attentive to the acceptable dress code at work.

You may limit your future by looking too much like a worker bee and not enough like a v.p. 'No, you look fine dressed like that,' is something a person says when they want to snag that next promotion ahead of you.

Jeans on a first date…mmm. They can come across as the sartorial equivalent of 'No effort made at all.'

Also remember that blue jeans can be hot and sticky in the summer and not that warm during the winter. This is the reason so many OMGs (Old Money Guys) roll with cotton pants in the spring and summer and corduroys through the winter and fall. Just sayin'.

Things to avoid: too tight jeans, torn jeans, and jeans that reveal the crack of your butt when you sit or bend over.

THE SHOES

THE CASUAL SHOE

Description: the casual shoe is a brown leather shoe or boot with a leather or rubber sole. A flip-flop is not considered a casual shoe.

History, if you care: about a week after the invention of the shoe, men with any choice in the matter probably decided that certain footwear was more suitable for physical work, and certain footwear was probably best reserved for dressy occasions.

This distinction of a work shoe and/or a dress shoe held for centuries, until the 1950s, when a generation of young men descended on college campuses, eager to learn and open to new ideas.

One of these new ideas was the casual shoe, a hybrid between a moccasin and a dress shoe. It had a leather upper like a dress shoe, but no shoelaces, and was cut low like the moccasin.

The penny loafer was the iconic model of the casual shoe during this time, accompanied by other slip-ons similar in design. The gentlemen students threw on their tweed jackets, button-down collar dress shirts, khakis, and loafers. They attended class, went to football games, and went to school dances in their versatile outfits and comfortable but appropriate casual shoes.

Almost 75 years later, the look and the logic of the casual shoe still holds.

Common colors & fabrics: most versatile in brown, most durable in leather.

Construction details: should be built to last with quality leather uppers, heavy stitching, sturdy leather or rubber soles, and comfortable in-soles.

Style parameters: round toe, traditional design that speaks more to function, durability and comfort than to elegance. The casual shoe can also be a brown leather shoe such as a moccasin, deck shoe, or chukka boot.

Best uses: the loafer (no laces) is a more casual piece of footwear that resides between the dress shoe and the athletic shoe. The penny loafer is an Old Money tradition, as is the deck shoe ('Topsider'). Both are welcome at the lobby bar, but if you're meeting someone special, go with the loafer. If you're slushing through snow, rock the boot.

The casual shoe elevates your look even if you're weekending with the polo shirt and khakis. A much better option that athletic shoes.

Usually worn with: the boot, loafer, or slip on can be worn with dress pants or casual pants. The topsider or moccasin should stay with casual pants and jeans.

Never worn with: the topsider or moccasin should never be worn with a suit. The penny loafers or slip ons can be worn with a suit, but it's not the most stylish ensemble.

Acceptable options: brown leather ankle boots or chukka boots with rubber soles can fill the same role. LL Bean and Allen Edmonds have a roster of casual brown shoes that can be paired with casual pants for a solid look.

If you only buy one: the polished brown leather loafer that can go dressy or casual, depending on your jacket and pants.

Preferred vendors: Mephisto, GH Bass, Allen Edmonds, Sperry, LL Bean.

How to care for it: polish, re-heel and re-sole as necessary. Purchase cedar shoe trees for all of your casual and dress shoes. The shoe trees will help maintain the shape of your shoes when they are not being worn, and the cedar will pull out the moisture, increasing the lifespan of the shoes.

Approximate price points: $150.00 to $400.00.

Things to remember: if you live in colder climates, your casual shoe may be a winter boot. If this is the case, look to Allen Edmonds and LL Bean for the best options at every price point.

Things to avoid: black loafers. Unless they're Gucci loafers, and only Gucci loafers in their classic, solid black leather model, when you can afford them. When you have purchased them, wear them everywhere and all the time. Wear the hell out of them. Climb Kilimanjaro in them. Because nothing looks more New Money than a nice, new pair of black Gucci loafers. I just want to spill a drink on them.

THE DRESS SHOE

Description: a lace-up leather shoe with leather sole in a traditional style.

History, if you care: the lace-up dress shoe worn by most men today is actually a product of Scotland. It is known as a Balmoral, named after the castle.

However, it wasn't until after the shoe became *de rigueur* at English prep schools—and became known as the Oxford—that the model gained broad acceptance, not only with men in the UK, but all over the world.

Along with its straightforward and straight-laced cousins, the wingtip, the brogue, and the derby, the Oxford dress shoe is the no-nonsense choice when it comes to footwear.

Black Oxfords have been worn by corporate titans and heads of state for the past century. They're elegant, clean, and discreet.

The dress shoe is what men have worn to communicate that they are to be taken seriously, and that they have style and taste.

Common colors & fabrics: always 100% cow leather. Best to go with brown, which is the most versatile. Black if you require a very formal look for finance, diplomacy, law, and politics.

Construction details: solid leather construction upper and leather sole. Three to six eyelets for thin brown or black shoe strings.

Style parameters: nothing two-tone. Nothing with a stacked heel or pointy toe. Nothing with a square toe. Nothing Elton John has worn on stage. Wingtips, brogues, or cap toe. Classic, timeless models only.

Best uses: taking care of business, looking like you mean business.

Usually worn with: the business suit, the blazer and dress pants, sometimes with casual pants, even jeans for an urban, dressy look.

Never worn with: the brown lace-up dress shoe doesn't really jive with linen pants.

Acceptable options: the monk strap or double monk are dress shoes with buckles. Not as formal as the lace-up, they make their own statement. A little more 'man of leisure' who still likes it elegant.

When the Benjamins hit the fan, treat yourself to the bespoke shoe experience. Edward Green upholds the British tradition. John Lobb is also a fine choice. Corthay in Paris caters to the daring.

If you only buy one: a chocolate brown lace-up from Allen Edmonds. The Strand and Park Avenue models are enduring classics.

Preferred vendors: Allen Edmonds.

How to care for it: polish, re-heel, and re-sole as needed. Purchase cedar shoe trees for all of your casual and dress shoes. The shoe trees will help maintain the shape of your shoes when they are not being worn, and the cedar will pull out the moisture, increasing the lifespan of the shoes.

Approximate price points: $400.00 to $500.00. Prices for bespoke dress shoes will make your think you're buying a very nice used car.

Things to remember: fewer pieces of your wardrobe are more important than your dress shoes. You will communicate volumes by selecting a well-crafted model in a classic style.

Buy the best you can afford and take care of them. Learn which size, brand, and style work for you. Watch for sales. Well made, well maintained shoes can last 20 years or more. Purchase with that in mind.

Things to avoid: exotic skins.

THE ATHLETIC SHOE

Description: the rubber sole shoe you wear to run, walk long distances, exercise, or play sports.

History, if you care: until the mid 1800s, shoes were almost always made of leather soles and uppers. A process known as vulcanization made it possible to join canvas and rubber together.

A few years later, the Goodyear company came out with Keds, the first sneaker, and in 1917 they finally started marketing the shoe as an athletic shoe.

In the following decades, new technologies and innovations transformed the athletic shoe. Fashion soon followed, with companies like Nike, Adidas, Puma, Reebok, and New Balance introducing colorful new designs and models at a dizzying pace.

In the 1970s, athletic shoes soon strolled off the court and into the street, becoming a daily, go-to footwear option for many men. Prices, too, have changed. Once an economical option for children and adolescents, athletic shoes for men can now cost several hundred dollars.

While the materials and styles have been updated to look more appealing, athletic shoes—referred to as sneakers or trainers—remain a too lax option for a gentleman to wear as a casual shoe.

Common colors & fabrics: the rainbow, synthetic fabrics, rubber, and leather.

Construction details: designed and built with rubber soles, sturdy fabrics and stitching to handle a lot of physical stress, pressure, and mileage.

Style parameters: best to stay with the classic white.

Best uses: should be worn when you're running or playing sports, going to or from the gym, or in the gym.

Usually worn with: sadly, too much of everything.

Never worn with: dress pants or a suit, please.

Acceptable options: the iconic Adidas three stripe All Star in white with black stripes, or the Stan Smith model in white with green trim, are the Old Money go-to's for walking the streets.

If you only buy one: the shoe that works for you when you're exercising, or the Adidas All Star.

Preferred vendor: Adidas.

How to care for it: moist cloth to wipe dirt away, bleach the shoe strings to regain like-new whiteness.

Approximate price points: $80.00 to whatever you want to spend.

Things to remember: sport your best look in even your most casual moments with a classic pair of white Adidas athletic shoes.

Things to avoid: spending $300.00 on sneakers. You look like a victim of marketing.

THE COATS

THE RAINCOAT

Description: a light to medium weight, full length coat to wear in wet and/or cold weather.

History, if you care: as straightforward and wonderful as the raincoat, or trench coat, is as an article of clothing, its origins seem to be equally as murky and controversial. So we'll take into consideration some history and make a small effort to sort things out.

The waterproof fabric used on many trench coats was apparently invented by Charles Mackintosh in 1823, and you can still buy a Mackintosh coat from the company today. Thomas Burberry (of today's Burberry luxury brand) invented gabardine fabric in 1879 and submitted a design to the British army for a trench coat in 1901. You can still buy a Burberry model today.

But wait. Aquascutum, another British luxury goods firm (Cary Grant was a famous client) claimed that it had designed the trench coat in 1850. And, yes, you can still buy an Aquascutum model today.

The debate about who actually invented the raincoat continues to rage. Okay, not exactly *rage*, but it continues, in that very civilized, British way.

Origins aside, the coats gradually made their way into British military attire, first with officers, then with all soldiers. The name 'trench coat' came into common use as soldiers wore these coats in the trenches during the first World War.

The coat cemented its current iconic style status when Humphrey Bogart wore one in the classic film *Casablanca* eighty years ago. The raincoat's elegance, fabric, and functionality remain timeless.

Common colors & fabrics: tan or grey, natural looking synthetic fibers.

Construction details: the models you want to look at will probably have a removable wool lining, giving the coat more life as temperatures fluctuate. The belt that comes with the raincoat or trench coat looks best tied, not buckled.

Style parameters: stick with the classic double breasted style in tan or eggshell. Length should be to the knee.

Best uses: when it's raining, obviously. This coat will protect you from the rain and project a classic, serious image, dress or casual.

Usually worn with: shoes or boots that are weather-worthy.

Never worn with: shorts.

Acceptable options: the London Fog Plymouth model in navy or black. The Mackintosh, made in Cumbernauld, Scotland and Nelson, Lancashire.

If you only buy one: the classic London Fog Raleigh model in khaki.

Preferred vendors: London Fog. Mackintosh.

How to care for it: dry clean only.

Approximate price points: $150.00 to $700.00.

Things to remember: if you live in a pedestrian city like New York or Boston, the trench coat or raincoat is standard equipment for commuting. Try it on in the store over your sport coat or suit coat. Give yourself room.

And for God's sake, man, turn that collar up.

Things to avoid: the shorter length. Your pants will just get wet.

THE OVERCOAT

Description: a full length wool coat for serious winter wear. This coat usually extends below the knee.

History, if you care: long coats that protect men from cold, rain, and snow have been around for centuries, and it would be pointless to try to pinpoint the origins of the garment.

That said, the model most resembling what we wear today probably originated in England in the late 18th century. At that point in time, the overcoat was worn much like gentlemen wear a suit coat today. It was tailored and fitted, denoting a certain status and formality, and was usually worn by professional or military men.

When the style found its way to the general public a few decades later, the overcoat grew to be a little looser in cut and less formal in design.

Today, overcoats are usually cut to accommodate a blazer, jacket, or suit coat underneath. While synthetic fabrics abound, the best fabric for the overcoat remains wool.

Common colors & fabrics: 100% wool, or a wool and cashmere blend. Tan or navy.

Construction details: heavy wool and silk lining, lightly-padded shoulders and front pockets for hands and gloves.

Style parameters: single or double breasted models, as you prefer. Length should be to the knee. Solid colors.

Best uses: for cold weather, but not really for extended exposure to snow or rain.

Usually worn with: corduroy pants or wool dress pants.

Never worn with: linen pants. Athletic wear.

Acceptable options: the navy blue pea coat, in a 3/4 length.

If you only buy one: the double-breasted Polo Coat in tan.

Preferred vendors: O'Connell's Clothing, Brooks Brothers, Ralph Lauren.

How to care for it: dry clean only.

Approximate price points: $1200.00 to $1800.00, but check vintage stores for great bargains on quality models.

Things to remember: try this coat on over your sport coat or suit coat to get the right size. It's okay if you throw the overcoat on over a sweater and it's a little loose. It's not okay if you throw it on over a jacket and it's a too tight.

In spring, summer, and fall, store this wool garment—and all wool garments—in canvas garment bags, not plastic. Remember: the fabric can't breathe in plastic.

Things to avoid: synthetic fabrics posing as wool overcoats.

THE WINTER COAT

Description: the winter coat that can endure cold, snow, and rain.

History, if you care: we'll have to acknowledge the original parka, an invention of the Caribou Inuit people, natives of the Canadian Arctic. They crafted their early coats from caribou or seal skin, and coated them with fish oil to make them water resistant.

Thankfully for us, the caribou, and the seals, times have changed. Recent developments in synthetic fabrics such as nylon and the use of goose down feathers have created incredibly warm, insulated, and waterproof coats to endure the harshest of cold and wet conditions.

Rest easy, animal lovers: even the fur trim around the hoods of these garments is now man-made.

Common colors & fabrics: navy blue and black are your best options, unless you have a expedition to Antartica on the schedule, in which case I believe a bright red is appropriate.

Construction details: filled with goose down feathers on the inside, what we're calling the 'winter coat' has a nylon or other synthetic fabric exterior which repels rain and snow with ease. A hood is standard equipment, with front pockets for hands and gloves, and interior pockets for the wallet and phone.

Style parameters: function trumps all here. The length is usually just below the hips, rarely to the knees. A fur-trimmed hood is common.

Best uses: when you must carry on in freezing temperatures that include precipitation. A great gift for that college freshman, especially when attending university in the northeast, as winters there can be brutal.

Usually worn with: wool sweaters, thermal underwear, lots of layers, anything that will keep you warm and dry.

Never worn with: any sense of elegance or style. You're just trying to survive the cold.

Acceptable options: The Triple F.A.T. Goose Eberly II is a good choice, with a longer length.

If you only buy one: The North Face Mcmurdo Parka in navy or black.

Preferred vendors: The North Face. Triple F.A.T. Goose.

How to care for it: wipe with damp cloth as needed. Do not use it as a sleeping bag.

Approximate price points: $350.00 to $650.00.

Things to remember: keep to navy or black, as the elements will leave their mark on other colors.

Things to avoid: fashion forward models of this coat. You'll look cool, but you won't be as warm.

THE GEAR

SPORTSWEAR

Description: these are the clothes you exercise or play sports in that are most often a long sleeve pullover or zip-front top and full length bottoms.

History: once limited to the clean and classic golf and tennis outfits to the very functional grey sweatshirt and sweatpants, sportswear has morphed into a billion dollar athletic-slash-casual wear industry in just a few short decades.

Natural fabrics, mostly cotton, have been largely replaced by lighter weight synthetic fabrics that absorb moisture more efficiently and dry more quickly.

With all these technical innovations, of course, come fashion faux pas: too-short shorts, colorful headbands, velour warmup suits, tank tops, and knee-high socks.

Happily, function has returned to the forefront, with athletic attire again designed to wear and work well, with a minimum of dizzying patterns and designs on the market. Sadly, logos and slogans dominate, but tomorrow is another day.

Common colors & fabrics: 100% cotton for the T-shits and sweats, to all manner of synthetic fabrics that can breathe and dry quickly for everything else.

Construction details: quality sportswear constructed of synthetic fabrics on the outside usually has a softer, cotton or cotton-like lining on the inside to absorb moisture and offer a layer of comfort against the skin. The minimum would be a mesh lining, like the kind often found in swimwear. Stitching should be sturdy to endure the stretching and stress of workouts. Draw strings, elastic, and zippers should be strong in order to keep the garments in place during exercise. Hoods and pockets are bonuses for foul weather and house keys.

Style parameters: keep these functional, with solid colors: black or grey if you workout during the day, or an bright orange or optic yellow if you need to be seen by automobiles in the evening. Limit the logos.

Best uses: when you are exercising or participating in an athletic activity and only then.

Usually worn with: athletic shoes.

Never worn with: house shoes.

Acceptable options: the 100% cotton hoodie and the nylon warmup suit for rain and cold.

If you only buy one: the classic 100% cotton grey sweatshirt, grey sweat pants, grey T-shirt, grey gym shorts.

Preferred vendors: Champion, Adidas.

How to care for it: machine wash per garment instructions.

Approximate price points: $20.00 to $200.00.

Things to remember: it's about being healthy, not making a fashion statement.

Things to avoid: wearing sportswear to a cafe, restaurant, or bar. Contrary to popular opinion, it is not a good choice.

SWIMWEAR

Description: the clothing you wear while swimming or sunbathing.

History, if you care: evolving from the striped, full-body 'tank suits' for men in the 1890s, men's swimwear has paired down over the last century. It now most often refers to simply 'swim trunks' that often resemble the boxers or briefs styles of men's underwear.

Common colors & fabrics: usually a synthetic, nylon fabric that is lightweight and dries quickly.

Construction details: synthetic, nylon-like fabrics dominate the market now. The Speedo-style swimsuits are designed to be worn snug, with reinforced elastic around the waist and legs. The surfer style trunks usually have a drawstring and elastic, with mesh or cotton-like lining for comfort. Both are designed with the intention of keeping the swimsuit in proper position, whether you're enjoying the big waves of Oahu or the cliff-diving in Acapulco.

Style parameters: swim trunks, which are looser fitting short pants, often worn by surfers, and the tighter 'Speedo' style briefs, often worn by Olympic swimmers, are the two basic options.

Best uses: to be worn only while at the pool, in the lake, at the beach, on the boat, or in the jacuzzi.

Usually worn with: sandals, slippers, or sneakers, and some kind of shirt or robe to cover up with.

Never worn with: unwarranted confidence.

Acceptable options: the retro, tight-fitting boxer-brief style trunk.

If you only buy one: a solid color or simple pattern swim trunk.

Preferred vendors: Speedo or any department store offering.

How to care for it: per garment instructions.

Approximate price points: $15.00 to $30.00.

Things to remember: if you're young, thin or in great condition, a 'Speedo' looks fine. If you're older or heavier, consider the trunks. No butt floss. Wear a shirt or bathrobe and slippers or shoes if you are leaving your hotel room and going to the hotel swimming pool. Cover up. Disrobe at the pool. Cover up on your way back to the room. The same goes for country clubs or public pools or beaches.

Things to avoid: wearing swim trunks to a cafe, bar, or restaurant. Contrary to popular opinion, it is not a good choice.

SLEEPWEAR

Description: the attire you wear while sleeping, or in the privacy of your own home near bedtime, or immediately after getting out of bed.

History if you care: pajamas, robes, and house slippers were initially invented to keep men warm while they slept in poorly insulated and poorly heated bedrooms. Over time, these garments evolved into comfortable, and even luxurious, garments to sleep in, and lounge around the house in.

Common colors & fabrics: solid color, 100% cotton pajamas are common, as is the 100% cotton, terry-cloth robe. Silk pajamas are an upscale option, with the velvet (collar and cuffs) and silk robe.

Construction details: pretty straightforward: long sleeves, long pants for the pajamas. The robe is a full cut. The slippers can be leather with fur lining, if you live in a colder climate. Also consider cotton or velvet.

Style parameters: these garments tend to be worn a little larger than daily wear fashions, allowing for comfort as you toss and turn in the bed at night. The slippers are more delicately constructed and soled, as they are not meant for street wear.

If you are suddenly *not* on a budget and would like to indulge, fly to London, check into the Sheraton Grand Park Lane, and wander over to Jermyn Street, where an eye-popping variety of luxury pajamas and robes awaits your review. The usual suspects include Turnbull and Asser and Derek Rose. For dressing gowns in particular, visit New and Lingwood.

Best uses: to be worn in your residence or hotel room only.

Usually worn with: the pajamas are often worn with the robe and slippers.

Never worn with: an overcoat, unless you want to look like you've just escaped from, you know, *the home.*

Acceptable options: The 100% cotton nightshirt, a billowy, one-piece garment, is also a nice option.

If you only buy one: long sleeve, long pants, 100% cotton pajamas in light blue, a navy or burgundy terry-cloth robe, and cotton house slippers.

Preferred vendors: high quality men's sleepwear is most reliably found in high-end department stores like Neiman Marcus, Bergdorf Goodman, and Saks Fifth Avenue.

How to care for it: machine wash, per garment instructions, and take care with the drying, as pajamas can shrink.

Approximate price points: $40.00 to $250.00 for pajamas. Robes and dressing gowns start at $50.00 and can go to $3500.00.

Things to remember: A luxurious, well-made set of pajamas, slippers, and robe is a private but quite satisfying reward for a man who's accomplished a worthwhile professional or financial goal. Fabrics can be embracing and workmanship enthralling. Something to consider when the year-end bonus arrives.

It's really important to keep your pajamas clean and fresh.

Things to avoid: letting the pajama bottoms ride too low.

ACCESSORIES

THE NECKTIE

Description: the necktie is a silk accessory that accompanies the shirt and jacket to give a man a more formal look.

History, if you care: various incarnations of the cravat or necktie have been around for centuries, probably beginning with Louis XIII. Being a king, he decided he needed some mercenaries from Croatia. Being French, he looked them over and decided they didn't quite have the *je ne sais quoi* he was going for. So he ordered them to wear a piece of silk fabric around their necks as a part of their uniforms, and christened them '*cravates*'.

As with all things necktie, the accessory soon became mandatory. And not just in France. Any serious gentleman in the last 200 years would throw on his jacket, vest, and cravat or necktie before stepping out to take care of business on the European continent or in the American colonies.

Today's necktie hasn't changed in its basic style or shape in about 100 years. It has assumed and held its present length, ending somewhere just north or south of a man's waist line.

It does, however, still fluctuate in width. The 1960s witnessed skinny ties. The 1970s, wide ties. And so it goes, back and forth every ten to fifteen years. It's like watching a tennis match in very slow motion. Back and forth. Over decades.

One thing remains unchanged: the necktie is the accessory that most accurately designates the relative importance or formality of the circumstances in which it's worn.

Common colors and fabrics: a go-to option for you is the navy blue, solid color, with small white dots, or a version with blue and white stripes. Every color of the rainbow and every patter imaginable have been manufactured and worn, with varying degrees of success. All good neckties are, however 100% silk.

Construction details: the exterior fabric is folded and wrapped around a lining, which gives the tie its shape and body.

Style parameters: proportion is key. Make sure the width of your jacket or suit lapels, your shirt lapels, and your necktie are comparable. A particular misery of mine is to see a man dressed in a moderately styled jacket with well-balanced lapels, coupled with a moderately styled shirt with appropriately sized collar, and a too-skinny necktie. Remember: proportion is key.

Best uses: when you want to show the upmost respect for the event you're going to attend or the person you're going to meet. Can be obligatory for many workplaces and formal social gatherings that include weddings, memorials, graduations, and many religious services.

Usually worn with: a suit or a jacket. Sometimes a just a sweater. (See the late, great Mr. Rogers from public television.)

Never worn with: just a vest.

Acceptable options: the bowtie, if you're feeling academic, cable news pundit-ty, or just plain rebellious in a traditional sort of way. Please note, however, that the bowtie must be hand-tied, unless it is from Charvet in Paris.

If you only buy one: The Brooks Brothers No 1 BB rep tie.

Preferred vendors: many designers make great ties at a variety of price points. Start with the basics at reasonable prices. When logic and budgetary constraints are on holiday, consider the multitude of fabulous offerings at Hermes and Charvet in Paris, and Turnbull and Asser in London.

How to care for it: dry clean only, and only if you get some pasta sauce on it.

Approximate price points: $30.00 to $175.00.

Things to remember: it's best to just tie a four-in-hand knot (see YouTube), pull it up reasonably tight and fairly centered, and forget about it. Having too big or too perfect of a tie knot is not a plan.

You have your quality garments. You have your ensembles for each occasion. You're now able to just give the old tie knot a rakish wrap and a pull, and forget about it. This will hint that you don't care that much about you look. You do care. You just don't let other people know that you care.

Things to avoid: being too clever with your tie, Christmas lights on your tie, political motifs on your tie, pinup girls on your tie, colors, patterns, symbols, slogans, or mascots that make people think or blink.

THE BELT

Description: usually a brown or black leather strap with metal buckle that, theoretically, holds your pants up, but more often than not is a decorative accessory for pants that have belt loops.

History, if you care: first used in ancient Egypt to keep those tunics under control in the desert wind, belts have served a primarily functional role in men's clothing history. While they may have been a handy place for Renaissance rogues to tuck away the odd sword or dagger, times have changed. Weapons aren't quite so necessary today, and with innovations in modern tailoring, most pants will stay up most of the time. Today, the belt is simply a subtle but essential accessory for the well-dressed man.

Common colors & fabrics: dark brown leather is best, as is a navy blue or brown woven cotton belt for more casual wear.

Construction details: best in cowhide, with a simple, thin buckle in silver or gold finish.

Style parameters: keep it thin, as western style belts won't fit through the belt loops of dress and casual pants. Keep it simple. Keep it understated.

Best uses: the belt is necessary if you're going to appear completely dressed.

Usually worn with: the leather belt is usually worn with suits, dress pants, and casual pants. The woven cotton belt is best with casual pants and jeans.

Never worn with: pants that don't have belt loops.

Acceptable options: for summer or more casual wear, the woven cotton belt with leather trim. Navy blue is the standard issue on this model.

If you only buy one: the brown cowhide leather belt with simple buckle.

Preferred vendors: Lands' End. Brooks Brothers.

How to care for it: don't swim in it. That would help.

Approximate price points: $40.00 to $60.00.

Things to remember: if you've got your look together, and you've got a worn out belt, you're shooting yourself in the foot. Keep a nice looking belt or two in your rotation. Keep the style simple. For bargains, visit a vintage store, but select only a belt that looks almost new.

Things to avoid: exotic skins. Reversible belts.

THE SOCKS

Description: the cotton or wool garments you wear on your feet to protect them against the leather of your shoes.

History, if you care: when leather met skin, blisters were born. Socks were invented shortly thereafter.

No, seriously…primitive socks made of clumped animal hair were worn by the ancient Greeks, who held them in place (sort of) with twine tied around their ankles. Thankfully, improvements followed, and we're lucky enough to have not been around for the innovations in between then and now. The knitting machine, invented in 1589, really helped the cause, as did the invention of elastic in 1820. Today, functional and stylish socks are available in a wide variety of fabrics, weights, and colors.

Common colors & fabrics: for our purposes, cotton or wool, although nylon is popular. Navy blue, black or chocolate brown.

Construction details: elastic upper to hold them against the leg, a smooth lower that form-fits around the foot.

Style parameters: for dress, socks are often designed to be worn over the calf, preventing that ghastly, gasp-inducing sight of a man's bare, hairy leg peeking out between the top of his sock and the bottom of his pants leg. Most socks are about 10 inches high. I won't even discuss ankle socks.

Best uses: should be worn anytime you step outside the house, with the exception of 'weekends' when you are off the clock. Then, feel free to slip into the loafers or Topsiders *sans chaussettes*. Wool socks are a good option as they dry much more quickly and are often thicker than their cotton counterparts.

Usually worn with: dress pants, casual pants.

Never worn with: pajamas, in bed.

Acceptable options: argyle socks are a jovial style option if you want to spice up a traditional ensemble. Best with loafers.

If you only buy one: a navy sock in a medium thickness (not too thin) that can offer some cushion as you stroll the streets in your loafers or dress shoes.

Preferred vendors: LL Bean for wool ragg socks. Pantherella for dress socks.

How to care for it: machine wash, tumble dry or hang dry.

Approximate price points: $10.00 to $30.00 per pair.

Things to remember: your socks should always be as dark or darker than your pants.

Things to avoid: pastel colored socks. Droopy socks, unless they're a massively thick wool.

THE SCARF

Description: a wool, cashmere, or cotton accessory worn around the neck to keep warm and/or look elegant.

History, if you care: the early versions of shirts were a tragic mess, and coats were incredibly rough and heavy. The scarf was invented to keep the neck and chest warm, and to buffer the skin against the unkind wool of the coat.

Common colors & fabrics: wool and cashmere are obvious choices for colder climates. Best, again, in the navy blue, tan, brown, dark green, or grey we've come to know and love. If you want to go crazy with something completely off the (color) charts, this is the accessory to do it with. Just don't do it with silk.

Construction details: the finer models have knotted fringe at each end. Luxury models may be silk on one side and cashmere on the other, with contrasting colors, and handcrafted fringe. For some reason, a scarf looks odd if it doesn't have fringe on each end.

Style parameters: the longer the better, in my opinion. You'll get finer fabrics and more beautiful color combinations when you explore finer retailers and pay more. That said, I've found some beautiful, well-made scarves here in Paris at the street markets, usually imported from India, for very reasonable prices.

Cotton scarves are a great style touch when it's just a little cool, or when you just want to look a little cool.

Best uses: scarves are best worn to keep your neck and chest warm first and foremost.

Usually worn with: scarves work best with tweed jackets and wool coats, and sometimes with just a wool sweater.

Never worn with: wool or cashmere scarves should never be worn with linen pants or linen jackets. Cotton scarves may be worn with linen.

Acceptable options: if you are attending a sporting event and your team really needs your support, I will allow you to wear your team's branded scarf. Just this once.

If you only buy one: the navy blue or tan 100% wool or cashmere scarf.

Preferred vendors: too numerous to mention. That said, don't be too proud to visit local vintage stores. You'll probably find some great scarves, in perfect condition, at a fraction of their retail price, just waiting to adorn your neck. At retail establishments, watch for off-season sales, usually in the early spring.

How to care for it: if it's been a really good party, and you wake up on the floor of a stranger's apartment, and are still wearing your scarf, you will want to have it dry cleaned. Always keep your wool scarves stored with your other wool garments in a canvas garment bag.

Approximate price points: $45.00 to $200.00.

Things to remember: this is another opportunity to look like you don't give a damn, or to actually not give a damn. Just grab that scarf and throw it around your neck and go!

Things to avoid: synthetic fabrics.

The Hat

Description: the hat is an accessory worn on your head to protect it from cold, rain, or sun. It is also used to express style.

History, if you care: hats have been worn throughout the ages and are more often worn in societies in which gender roles are more defined. In the last 70 years, wearing a hat daily has decreased dramatically and is now limited to keeping your head warm and dry.

The popular men's dress hat, the fedora, was originally made for women. Legendary actress Sarah Bernhardt wore a soft-brimmed model in a play entitled, 'Fedora'. Forty years later, Prince Edward of Britain started wearing a fedora, and the style became accepted worldwide. Part of the popularity was fashion, part of it was function, as the fedora was also pretty good at keeping a man's head warm and dry.

The Panama hat is made in Ecuador, actually, but their original point of sale to international markets was Panama, hence the name. Introduced to the general public at the world's fair in 1855, the hat went viral when President Theodore Roosevelt was photographed wearing one when he visited the Panama Canal in 1906.

The beret has been around for centuries in various incarnations, but the version we see today probably has its origins in the Basque region, circa 1600. The French military adopted berets as part of their uniforms in the late 1800s. Artists, writers—and guys posing as artists and writers in order to seduce women—have worn the beret for the last century.

The 'newsboy', a wool cap popular in the early 20th century with boys who sold newspapers and others of the working class, has made a comeback in recent years. Warm and weather-worthy, it's inherently casual, but a classic.

Common colors & fabrics: felt, straw, wool, cotton, in every color of the rainbow.

Construction details: depends on the hat.

Style parameters: the fedora is the iconic, dressy model, which can be constructed with wool, cashmere, or beaver. Chocolate brown, navy, or dark green will serve you best. Expensive, better-made fedoras are lined in silk. If you dress for work (suit and tie) or want to get your look on at the racetrack, wear this with an overcoat if it's chilly, with the blazer or tweed jacket, dress pants, and dress shoes.

Quality equals price more acutely with the Panama hat than almost any other hat, with the top end products feeling more like a cotton fabric than a straw. Often crafted in the same style as the fedora, Panama hats are for spring and summer. Keep the hat band black with this model, and, aside from the blue blazer, wear only linen or cotton with it. The Montecristi model is the ultimate (superfino), with the tightest weave, and is priced accordingly.

The beret is the underused option for American men, as it keeps your head warm like the knit cap and can repel rain almost as well as the fedora. Also, it's less likely to be blown off your head by a gust of wind. It can also be shoved inside a coat pocket when you arrive at the cafe. The beret is a navy blue or black wool, with a silk lining. Borsalino is an Italian firm that manufactures a quality model. Wear it, pushed to one side, with a scarf and coat, and you'll be warm and look great.

A classic cap is the newsboy (or the 'casquette' in French), which is best in wool. It has a stiff brim on the front which the fabric is usually snapped onto. These are a jaunty, durable option, especially when paired with the tweed jacket. Clever young gents will want to wear this one backwards, which is easy to do, but tricky to do well. The Harris tweed models are ubiquitous in England, Scotland, Ireland, and northern France. To see a veritable banquet of these caps and what they're worn well with, enjoy the classic film, *The Quiet Man* starring John Wayne.

The knit cap is a go-to option for very cold weather. It has nothing to offer style-wise, but I've heard it is functional.

With even less to offer is the baseball cap. If you must wear one, find a Ralph Lauren or Brooks Brothers model with a subtle logo on it, and leave it at that. (Remember my suggestions on logos: keep them small and discreet.)

Best uses: gentlemen, we need to keep exposure to the sun to a minimum. It wrinkles and spots the skin prematurely and can contribute to more serious skin conditions. Learn to wear the appropriate hat when you're going to be at an outdoor event, or exposed to the elements. Hats will protect your skin, and health is a big part of Old Money Style.

And take your damn hat off when you go indoors, especially at restaurants, and especially when you are introduced to a lady.

Usually worn with: a fedora should be worn with a jacket, dressier pants, and dressier shoes. The same goes for the straw hat. The beret works best with a scarf and jacket or coat. That said, I recently saw a young man with a blue blazer, khakis, button-down and rep tie, sporting his Brooks Brothers baseball cap. Not a bad look, I must admit.

Never worn with: unless it's the baseball cap or knit cap, never wear a hat with sportswear.

Acceptable options: we've covered more than a few.

If you only buy one: the black beret by Borsalino.

Preferred vendors: find a brick-and-mortar milliner (hat shop) or men's clothing boutique in your area and pay a visit. Otherwise, an upscale department store may be a source, especially if you live in New York, Boston, Chicago, or Washington, DC.

How to care for it: gentle brush for the fedora, avoiding rain for the straw.

Approximate price points: $40.00 to $500.00.

Things to remember: the right hat can protect your skin, keep you warm, and add a touch of style to your ensemble. Choose with care.

Things to avoid: cowboy hats, unless you actually own cattle and horses. Top hats, unless you are actually attending the races at Ascot. Bowlers.

JEWELRY

Description: the rings, necklaces, bracelets, wristwatch, pocket watch, or cufflinks that a man wears when he's dressed.

History, if you care: for the last 75,000 years (who's counting?), jewelry has been used to communicate social status, wealth, and position. Ancient texts, archives, and historical portraits testify to a veritable bling-fest, lasting centuries and including merchants, monarchs, popes and pirates, all going for the gold in the freestyle jewelry event.

In addition to impressing others with displays of affluence, jewelry was a sometimes practical way to store and transport wealth, especially in dicey political climates. A man might need to grab a sandwich, hop on a horse, and make a run for the border if a coup brought the current government down. In these circumstances, it might be a good thing to have a portable, highly liquid form of wealth that he could slip on and off, conceal beneath clothing, and use to cushion his landing in a new region, or a new country.

The signet ring, one with an official seal or family crest engraved upon it, was sometimes used as a signature, allowing at the wearer to press the engraved design into hot wax and authenticate a document.

Today, political conditions are slightly more stable, and notaries put their seal on important documents. Clothing, cars, houses, and corner offices convey wealth, position, and status. You'd think men's compulsion for wearing conspicuous jewelry would ebb. But no.

Nevertheless, let's agree that jewelry requirements for the civilized, 21st century man have been distilled to the wedding band and the wristwatch. The wedding band conveys marital status and the wristwatch tells time.

In the past 40 years, the wristwatch has evolved into a status symbol, but the temptation to mimic common behavior has been moderated by the good judgment, taste and discretion of gentlemen.

Only those blessed or burdened with hereditary titles bother to wear signet rings engraved with their family crest. Everyone else keeps it clean.

Common colors & materials: gold, platinum, and silver are the most common metals used in jewelry. Precious stones are also common in men's jewelry. Sadly, turquoise has happened.

Construction details: for most well-dressed men, jewelry pieces are constructed to fit fingers, wrists, or to be worn around the neck.

Style parameters: if you're married, feel free to wear a gold or platinum wedding band on your ring (third) finger of your left hand. If you like to wear a wrist watch, wear that.

Best uses: a little gold goes a long way on a man. To try to communicate wealth or status by wearing jewelry in public is antithetical to the Old Money culture. Don't do it.

Again, if you're married, you may wear a wedding band on your third finger. If you don't like looking at your phone to know the time, you may wear a wristwatch. Perhaps you wear a thin gold necklace underneath your dress shirt because it has religious or sentimental meaning to you. Good. Stop. Doing anything more is tricky business.

Usually worn with: all of your dress and casual outfits.

Never worn with: swimwear or sportswear.

Acceptable options: the military or university class ring. The pocket watch. The sports watch.

If you only buy one: your wedding ring. For watches, I have to increase the selection to three: a stainless steel Rolex, a Cartier tank watch with black leather band, or a Timex Waterbury Classic Chronograph. Clean. Classic. Simple. Timeless.

Preferred vendors: Rolex, Cartier, or a reputable vintage jewelry vendor, and the Timex website.

How to care for it: have your timepiece cleaned and checked at a reputable repair shop every 18 months to two years on the Rolex and Cartier models. Change the battery as needed on the Timex.

Approximate price points: $100.00 to $10,000.

Things to remember: your jewelry is about how subtly you're able to communicate your social status, if you communicate anything at all. Your wristwatch should reflect discretion, taste, and modesty. It should whisper, not shout.

Just keep the design classic. The strap should be a black or brown leather, or a grosgrain cotton band with blue/green or blue/red stripes.

Things to avoid: big gold watches. Big gold bracelets. Big gold necklaces. Big gold rings.

Eyeglasses and Sunglasses

Description: eyeglasses to help you see, and sunglasses to limit undue exposure to the rays of the sun.

History, if you care: for a few centuries now, eyeglasses have helped refract light rays so that they hit on the optic nerve, giving us clear vision (if I remember my 7th grade science lessons correctly).

Sunglasses, invented in the early part of the 20th century, became popular after movie stars started wearing them.

The first pair of wearable eyeglasses was thought to have been invented in the 1200s in Italy. The Spanish contributed eyeglass temples in the 1600s. In 1730, an optician named Edward Scarlett created the first rigid temples to rest on a person's ears, and hold the eyeglasses in place. And in 1784, Benjamin Franklin invented bifocals. Some people have been using them to look down their noses at other people ever since.

The monocle was a dashing innovation for men. The name, probably a derivative of the Latin word monoculus (one-eyed), was popular in the mid 1800s. When not in use, men let the lens hang using an elegant silk string or a gold or silver chain. Frames for monocles were made of animal bone or horn, and the eyepiece was not inexpensive. Bankers, horse breeders, lawyers, and politicians sported them, often with great affectation, as did more than a few Hollywood villains in black and white films.

The monocle was soon replaced by the pince-nez (French for 'pinched nose'), a set of lenses in a metal frame that offered corrective lenses for both eyes. If you paid attention in history class, you might remember photos of President Theodore Roosevelt, who often wore a pince-nez.

If you're a literary buff, you might recall Arthur Conan Doyle's *The Adventures of the Golden Pince-Nez*, one of the Sherlock Holmes short stories he published in 1904. The legacies of President Roosevelt and Sir Arthur Conan Doyle are still with us today. The pince-nez, not so much.

Today, eyeglasses come in a wide variety of styles and colors, and can be designed, measured, and fitted to look good and be comfortable for all-day wear.

Contact lenses and corrective surgeries are also options.

Common colors & fabrics: traditional sunglasses have gold, silver, brown, or black frames, and amber, dark green, or even yellow tinted lenses, which can be prescription or just 'off the rack', with no corrective function. Eyeglasses have just as many options in terms of frame styles and colors, and are most often made with clear prescription lenses.

Construction details: the lenses are now made of plastic. The temples are the parts of the eyeglasses that run along each side of your head and hold your eyeglass frames in place. They are most often made of acetate. Cellulose acetate, extravagantly known as the 'caviar of plastics', is the top of the line. Durable and hypoallergenic, it holds colors exceptionally well, in case anyone ever asks.

Style parameters: a few brands for eyeglasses and sunglasses set the standards and define the styles for this sometimes essential accessory. Warby Parker sells sunglasses and eyeglasses online. A great choice for quality and value.

When price is less of a consideration, Ray-ban and Persol dominate the (tasteful) market sector with their classic designs and predictable high quality.

Other manufacturers often mimic their iconic styles, with varying degrees of success. If you have black, grey, silver, or white hair, consider black frames. If you have brown or blonde hair, lean toward the tortoise shell look or brown. (See my comments about 'tortoise shell' below.)

Best uses: if you're like me and can't see your hand in front of your face, much less a street sign at the corner, it's best to wear your eyeglasses or contacts at all times. Sunglasses should be worn outdoors when the sun is actually out. Otherwise people might think you're taking yourself too seriously.

Usually worn with: everything.

Never worn with: Venetian carnival masks.

Acceptable options: as a very personal choice, eyeglasses need to reflect your personal style and accommodate your budget. For sunglasses, the wrap-around style are fine for sports and riding in one of those airboats that speeds through the Everglades.

If you only buy one: for sunglasses, Ray-ban's Original Wayfarer Classic.

Preferred vendors: Ray-ban, Persol, Warby Parker.

How to care for it: small screwdriver will keep the frames tight enough to keep the glasses from sliding down on your nose. The small tissue inside your eyeglass case will keep them clean.

Approximate price points: $120.00 to $350.00.

Things to remember: sunglasses do protect your eyes from damaging and uncomfortable sunlight. They also limit communication between people, so, if you're having a conversation with someone, take your sunglasses off. Other people need to know that you're listening, and that you understand them.

Likewise, if you're sitting at a sidewalk cafe in Rome and the *bella donna* you're trying to charm never takes her sunglasses off, wish her the best, pay the bill, and go throw a coin in the Trevi fountain. She's not interested.

Things to avoid: tinted eyeglasses. They engender distrust.

Also avoid frames made from endangered species, specifically the hawksbill sea turtle.

As someone who's embracing Old Money Style, you're going to be encouraged to do so without doing unnecessary harm to the planet or the animals that we share it with.

Turtles are one of those animals. The tortoise shell has been a luxurious, prized material since the time of the ancient Egyptians. Two hundred years ago, finer homes had tortoise shell combs, letter openers, cigar boxes, and even ice buckets for champagne.

That was then. This is now. The hawksbill sea turtle is on the endangered species list, and all species of turtle are being threatened with the volume of garbage that's in the ocean, coastal real estate development, and global warming. In spite of all this, some upscale boutiques still offer authentic tortoise shell sunglasses and eyeglasses, harvested from living animals.

With the availability, durability, and look of acetate frames, there's no reason to purchase tortoise shell frames. Don't do it.

Purchase tortoise shell frames made of custom cellulose acetate. Eyeglass designers can concoct tortoise hues of every shade without any undue cruelty to animals.

THE HANDKERCHIEF

Description: a cotton square of hemmed fabric, usually white, often found in a gentleman's exterior jacket pocket for decoration, and in the interior pocket for utility.

History, if you care: originally referred to as a 'kerchief', it's an English innovation used by royalty and the aristocracy to wipe their noses and faces. Not what you'd intuitively think of as 'classy', but surprisingly functional in daily life.

With more casual attire creeping into modern, everyday life, men don't wear a jacket which could accommodate a handkerchief as often.

This is a small tragedy, but one that can be avoided by, first, wearing a jacket, and second, carrying a handkerchief in the pocket of said jacket.

Common colors & fabrics: 100% cotton and white, or blue and white checks or stripes.

Construction details: thin cotton fabric, about 12 inches by 12 inches, with hemmed borders. Often monogrammed.

Style parameters: note that the handkerchief can be used to wipe your brow and nose, clean your eyeglasses, or dry her tears. It can also be used for decorative purposes, if you fold it or just bunch it up and shove it in the exterior breast pocket of your blazer, jacket, or suit coat.

The *pocket square*, however, is usually 100% silk, and may be smaller than a handkerchief. The pocket square is solely for decorative purposes, i.e., to add a dash of color and elegance to your ensemble by resting nonchalantly in your jacket's exterior breast pocket.

It's important to know the difference between a handkerchief and a pocket square. I'm not sure why it's important, but it's one of those small distinctions gentlemen make.

If you wear your navy blazer and tweed jacket as your go-to upgrades, feel free to splurge on a dozen pocket squares in a variety of colors to add a pop of color and surprise to the classic ensembles you've curated.

Best uses: when you purchase a blazer, tweed jacket, or suit jacket, spray your favorite fragrance on a handkerchief and stick in in the interior breast pocket. It will smell delightful when you pull it out and offer it to a lady.

Keep your pocket squares folded and orderly in a drawer, and choose one that matches your mood and the occasion, prior to leaving the house.

Usually worn with: blazers, jackets, suits.

Never used as: a dinner napkin.

Acceptable options: paper tissues, if that's all you have.

If you only buy one: the classic white 100% cotton handkerchief.

Preferred vendors: Woods Linen of London.

How to care for it: machine wash and dry. Lightly bleach to bump up the whiteness.

Approximate price points: $5.00 to $20.00 for cotton handkerchiefs. $15.00 to $150.00 for silk pocket squares.

Things to remember: to carry a handkerchief at all times is one mark of a gentleman. Adopt this practice. Be willing to offer it to someone in need without hesitation. Do not give a damn about getting it back. Should you offer a handkerchief to a lady, you will be delighted when she asks for your contact information…because she'll need to wash your handkerchief and return it to you, of course. When this happens, well, *game on.*

Things to avoid: not having a handkerchief in your pocket. Not having a handkerchief or pocket square in your exterior jacket pocket.

GALLERY

The Uniform. The navy blazer, white shirt, rep tie, and grey slacks is your go-to ensemble for a multitude of occasions. Wear this with the brown lace-ups or loafers, and the world is your oyster.

Notice the length of the jacket: your fingers should be able to just curl up under the tail. If the jacket is finger-tip length, it's too long. If it's the same length as your jacket sleeves, it's too short. Also note the 1/4" of shirt sleeve showing beyond the jacket sleeve. This is optimal.

Photo courtesy of Brooks Brothers.

From O'Connell's Clothing in Buffalo, New York, the Travel Blazer is one of several blue blazers the firm offers. As the name implies, this garment is designed and constructed for convenience and comfort, with a multitude of pockets, no padding in the shoulders, and a fabric weave that positively laughs at the idea of wrinkles. Note: there is no law against owning more than one blue blazer.

Photo courtesy of the fine gentlemen at O'Connell's.
www.oconnellsclothing.com

A casual, contemporary take on the classic ensemble of blue blazer and khakis. This time with a grey turtleneck sweater and ankle
boots. Also note that the young man is reading a book, not looking
at his phone.

Photo courtesy of Senivpetro at Freepik.

Dressed to impress. The tweed jacket with necktie and sweater is a timeless tradition. Perfect and proper.

Photos courtesy of our friends at
Harris Tweed, Isle of Harris. Scotland.

The tweed jacket, wool sweater, dress shirt, and corduroy pants are the go-to items for a casual upgrade. This is also the best look for travel: comfortable, but not sloppy, with jacket pockets for the wallet, passport, and phone.

Photos courtesy of our friends at
Harris Tweed, Isle of Harris. Scotland.

Like I've always said, you can't be afraid of a little color. Definitely casual, this bomber jacket, and sweater combination is best for the weekends. The jeans are tighter than I recommend, but, overall, it's a great look for young men.

Photo courtesy of Senivpetro at Freepik.

The Ralph Lauren short sleeve polo shirt, layered and solo, in a variety of colors. These guys are models, so of course they look good in this classic. The good news is that you will, too.

Photo courtesy of Ralph Lauren.

The iconic Mercer and Sons Oxford Cloth Button Down Shirt. Durable, timeless, a great investment. A handwritten thank you note is included with each order. Rather classy. The biggest problem with these shirts is keeping them for yourself: wives and girlfriends-at-a-certain-stage-in-the-relationship have been known to pillage the gentleman's closet and wear his Mercer shirts with impunity on lazy Saturday mornings. You have been warned.

Photo courtesy of David Mercer at Mercer and Sons.
www.mercerandsons.com

The black lace up dress shoe, a little more casual with the tan sole. Worn with a pair of jeans, it's not a look I recommend. Brown shoes with jeans, khakis, and cotton pants. Black shoes are best with navy, grey, or black suits.

Photo courtesy of Freepik.

The Allen Edmonds Strandmok in brown with durable rubber sole is a great option for a casual shoe. Appropriate with jeans, chinos, or corduroys, your casual shoe should look good and wear well, regardless of the weather, years, or mileage.

Photo courtesy of the fine gentlemen at Bespoke Unit.
www.bespokeunit.com

Allen Edmonds Strand model dress shoe in brown, a timeless, elegant, sturdy, and loyal fixture in the gentleman's wardrobe. The design, construction and style will serve you well. The Strand is perfect for suits, dress slacks, chinos, or even jeans. This shoe would have been perfectly acceptable 50 years ago, and it will be perfectly acceptable 50 years from now.

Photo courtesy of Allen Edmonds www.allenedmonds.com

The Allen Edmonds Strand model dress shoe in brown, a timeless, elegant, and loyal fixture in the gentleman's wardrobe. The dressier Strand is perfect for suits, dress slacks, or chinos, but can work with jeans, as this image makes clear.

Photo courtesy of Allen Edmonds www.allenedmonds.com

Two options for overcoats, one in navy blue and one in tan. Not an inexpensive acquisition, but know that the author has owned and worn his wool overcoat for more than 30 years. Invest in quality. Take care of the garment. You'll save money in the long run.

Photo courtesy of the fine gentlemen at O'Connell's Clothing, Buffalo, New York.

The classic Cartier tank watch and the enduring stainless steel Rolex. If you want to communicate a lot with a little, wearing either of these two iconic timepieces is the way to do it. Remember: purchase new from an authorized dealer, or used from a reputable vintage watch store. Given the cost of this investment, I would recommend walking into a brick and mortar store, trying on the watch, and then considering a purchase. Deals online that are too good to be true are just that.

Photo courtesy of Cartier. Photo courtesy of Rolex.

Houston heart surgeon Dr. Mike Sweeney (right) raises a glass during a pheasant hunt in Wyoming. The traditional tweed jacket—and perhaps the beverage of choice—help keep him warm. To your health, Doctor.

Photo courtesy of Laura Sweeney.

Austin area nurse Roy Thomas wears hospital scrubs throughout the work week. Ready for a weekend brunch, he rolls relaxed and refined with a white shirt, blue cords, and grey jacket. The brown boots substitute nicely for penny loafers, and are perfect for Texas' unpredictable weather.

Photo courtesy of Darla Thomas.

Dr. Alan Tran, M.D., is elegant and at ease with the classic navy blue blazer and grey slacks combination. He enjoyed a comfortable childhood in the affluent District One of Saigon, Vietnam. However, at the age of nine, his family had to flee the country on a military transport. Two weeks later, the republic fell to communism, and, with all of their worldly possessions in three suitcases, they arrived in Oklahoma. As a student, the young Alan Tran first mastered English, then medicine. Today, he manages a successful medical practice in Southern California. In typical Old Money Style, Dr. Tran spends one day a week doing Cleft Lip and Palate reconstructive surgeries—free of charge—for underprivileged children.

Photo courtesy of Dr. Alan Tran.

Relaxed in the Pennsylvania countryside, Dennis DiLabio is ready for any weather in this layered ensemble of blue shirt, red tie, navy sweater, and tan jacket and pants. Note: the brown all-weather boots are a functional and appropriate choice for colder and wetter climates. Also note that the crewneck sweater works just fine with a necktie.

Photo courtesy of Dennis Dilabio.

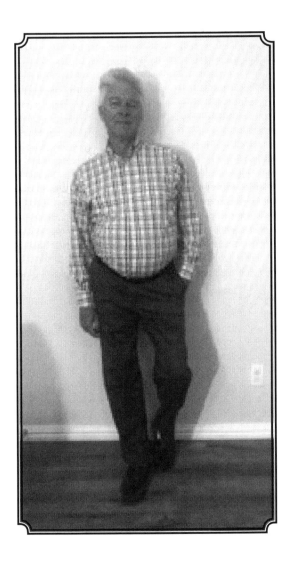

Dallas area high school teacher, tennis coach, and Methodist minister Brad Crawford often works long, 12-hour days. Like many Old Money Guys, he keeps it simple with a button-down collar shirt and khakis. A blue blazer— and a parent-teacher meeting—are probably close at hand.

Photos courtesy of Dr. Debi Crawford.

Singer songwriter Niels Brinck sports the gear for a run in the country. Remember: it's about exercising consistently and being healthy, not about what your'e wearing when you do it.

At ease, soldier. Former United States Marine Corps Sergeant Major Michael Sprue (retired), is now an executive in the tech sector. He rolls with casual comfort—and a fruity umbrella drink—in a short-sleeved shirt with collar. For sun protection, a discreet cap.

Then, for an elegant evening out, a shawl collar tuxedo. Note how well-trimmed his beard and mustache are in the casual photo, and the clean black and white of the formal ensemble. It's the details, gentlemen.

Photos courtesy of Candayce Spruel.

Keith Sinor, Houston area businessman, dressed for a lunch meet-ing. As Chief Financial Officer for his family business, he and his brothers are the 3rd generation at the helm. In typical Old Money Style, he serves on the board of trustees at the local community college and, with his wife Rae, chairs a private charitable founda-tion benefiting veterans and inner city children.

Photo courtesy of Rae Sinor.

This is not Old Money Style. This is what happens when you tell your friends you're writing a book on Old Money Style.

Photo courtesy of Rae Sinor.

It's important to remember that 'traditional' clothing means different things to different people around the world. Ike Anya, who,
with his wife, owns a Houston area construction company, rocks
traditional Nigerian attire with ease. During the week, however,
where his work takes him from building site to vendor showroom
to client lunch, you'll find him sporting Old Money Style with equal
aplomb.

If you're not giving, you're not living. Dr. Debi Crawford and husband Brad put their money where their hearts are. On this particular evening, they attend a gala fundraiser for Austin Angels, a nonprofit organization that supports children and parents in the foster care system. www.austinangels.com

Photo courtesy of Austin Angels.

Drew Walsh of London, Ontario, rolls out two easy and elegant options with the distinctive, hand-knotted bowtie. A tweed jacket with yellow sweater and navy wool pants, at top.

Now, with the King's College blue blazer, straw boater, and white wool pants. Well done, sir.

Photos courtesy of Drew Walsh.

Tech consultant and classic car enthusiast Clive Twyman rolls with the blue blazer, white dress shirt, tan pants, and brown loafers. The classic ensemble is the perfect backdrop for his necktie, which provides the perfect splash of color.

Art historian and author Dan Carrel knows his Monet's from his Manet's, and is passionate about the transformational power of art. His signature blue-on-blue shirt and tie combination is a great look, especially with the dramatic black suit.

Photo courtesy of Annie Lockhart.

Attorney James J. Gigliotti of Orlando, Florida, presents a timeless, professional look. The ensemble is composed entirely of high-quality Off The Rack garments, with minor alterations to the jacket and slacks by a skilled tailor. The fit is not too baggy, not too tight. The earth-tone colors combination with jackets and slacks whisper quietly and confidently. They also allow for multiple mix and match possibilities, making a few garments go a long way each week.

Photo courtesy of James J. Gigliotti.

Here, James executes the Daily Dress effortlessly with the blue blazer, a Brooks Brothers shirt and tie, O'Connell's poplin trousers, brown belt, and brown loafers. In typical Old Money Style, the stainless steel Rolex is worn discreetly under the shirt cuff. No need to advertise.

Photo courtesy of James J. Gigliotti.

Dennis DiLabio is quite well-dressed and ready for any weather in this layered ensemble of shirt, tie, sweater, and jacket. Note: the brown all-weather boots are a functional and appropriate choice for colder and wetter climates.

Photo courtesy of Dennis DiLabio.

Dr. Alan Tran is read for a formal evening in a tropical climate. His white dinner jacket is a shawl-collar model, and the shoes are patent leather formal slippers. Know that the substance is equal to the style: in addition to his charitable work, the good doctor is establishing My Viet Heritage, a cultural center to preserve and exhibit South Vietnamese artifacts, publications, and literature once in danger of being destroyed during and after the communists invasion of his country.

Photo courtesy of Dr. Alan Tran.

The Usual Suspects were detained by the Style Police of Florence, Italy, prior to a visit to the Accademia. Charged with not displaying sufficient 'bella figura' in the city, the group was let off with a warning, but had to pay a hefty fine for the cargo shorts.

Photo courtesy of Barbara Shallue.

Part III

Personal Grooming

THE FRAGRANCE

Description: the scent you wear to provide a pleasant smell for you and those who get close to you.

History, if you care: probably a French innovation from 3 or 4 centuries ago. People bathed maybe once a week back then, if at all. You can imagine.

Common scents: citrus, woodsy, floral.

Best uses: for cologne, a light spray right after a shower.

The fragrance is worn to enhance your presentation to those who will be within three feet of your person. Note that it is not to be detected by those people ten feet away from you, or worn so that people can smell you before they actually see you. Once again, 'subtle' is an appropriate adjective here.

Fragrance is not a substitute for hygiene. It is still important to shower or bathe, and use deodorant.

If your profession involves physically demanding work, you can use a little more fragrance or a heavier scent, or consider wearing a T-shirt under your uniform or dress shirt to conceal natural body odor.

If you only buy one: there are so many great colognes on the market, it's impossible to recommend just one. However, Pasha by Cartier and Aqua de Parma are classics.

Preferred vendors: Cartier boutiques and finer retail stores. For a unique experience, visit the lovely Marina Jung of ABC du Parfum and have a custom scent created especially for you and you alone in the privacy of her lovely 16th arrondissement apartment in Paris. *Tres chic.*

Approximate price points: $15.00 to $120.00.

Things to remember: you want to find a scent that will last throughout the day without overwhelming.

Things to avoid: cheaper brands.

THE HAIR

Description: your haircut and your facial hair.

History, if you care: a preoccupation and even obsession for men throughout the centuries. Powdered wigs reigned supreme for a number of years, followed by a brief intermission in the 20th century in which men simply lived with what they had (or didn't have).

Recent technological developments and changing cultural mores have led men to embrace hair color, for those going grey, and hair replacement, for those experiencing hair loss.

Construction details: Some men are blessed with a mane to die for. Some have an unruly, messy mop. And some, like me, well, we just have to work with what's left.

Style parameters: the mainstream, appropriate length of a man's hair for most professions and lifestyles hasn't really changed in the last 100 years. For guidance and inspiration, look at photos of the dignified Sidney Poitier, the charismatic Robert F. Kennedy, the inspiring Martin Luther King, the elegant Cary Grant, and legendary Franklin D. Roosevelt.

Part your hair on the left, part it on the right, or comb it straight back, and it will probably look fine. Parting it in the middle or combing it completely forward is trickier business.

Coloring your hair is also tricky business, and is best done by a really talented professional at a salon, on a regular basis. Pay for this.

If your hair is thinning, give it a nice, close trim. If you have the head and face for it, rock the bald look. If you feel it's important to have a full head of hair, you can consider single-follicle replacement procedures. Consult a talented physician for this, and only book an appointment through a referral. The referral would be from someone who has had the procedure done, and his results look natural and undetectable.

Best practices: find a talented barber or stylist who can assess the shape of your head and face and give you a cut that works. Once you've found it, stay with it, and forget about it. Healthy hair is a combination of diet, quality shampoos and conditioners, and an active lifestyle with moderated stress.

Organic castor oil applied regularly to the scalp is known to help slow hair loss, reinvigorate hair follicles, and return grey or white hair to its original color.

If you look great with a mustache, you know it. People have told you that you look great with a mustache, and you're fine taking care of your mustache so it always looks good and doesn't act as a facial attic for food particles. Rock the mustache.

If you have a great-looking Van Dyke (a mustache and chin-only beard), you know it. People have told you that you look great with a Van Dyke, even though they may refer to it inaccurately as a goatee. Keep your Van Dyke trimmed, healthy and clean. Know, however, that an actual goatee is not a solid choice.

If you have a great-looking full beard, you know it. People have told you it looks great. Be aware of your profession, however, as you sport your lumberjack look: people intuitively trust those with facial hair less than those without facial hair. If you're a college professor, you'll probably be fine. If you're a financial advisor, rethink the choice. If you keep it, maintain it. Please don't try to color it.

Approximate price points: good haircuts can be hard to find. Pay for a good cut if you can, every 4 to 6 weeks.

Things to remember: your hair should not be a distraction, to you or to others. Keep it neat. Keep it tight. Keep it healthy.

Eyebrows: there should be two. If your barber or stylist offers to trim your eyebrows, accept the offer. It's really a hint. As you age, hair may disappear from the top of your head and reappear inside your ears. Be vigilant. Keep ear hairs plucked.

Things to avoid: too much product in your hair. Ponytails. Unkept braids. Over-the-top and neglected dreadlocks. Sideburns below the middle ear.

HANDS AND FEET

Description: those things at the end of your arms and legs.

Best practices: caring for your hands and feet is not just ladies' business. Your nails must be cleaned daily, even if you do manual labor. Your cuticles need attention on a regular basis: trim them and use a good quality hand cream (not lotion) to soften and smooth rough edges.

Discover the healing and nourishing properties of organic shea butter, rosehip seed oil and marula oil. Avoid hand creams with parabens and other harmful ingredients.

Avoid fingernail polish, but consider buffing if you're at the executive level. This gives your fingernails a polished look without the polish. You can't be elegantly dressed and have mangled claws. It just don't work, bro.

Take care of your toenails as well. Use a pumice stone to buff the dead skin and callouses on your feet to give them a smooth feel. Don't wait until you slice open the bed sheet to notice that your toenails need trimming and filing. Treat yourself to a pedicure several times a year.

My own personal opinion is that God was really in top form when She created our head, our heart, arms and hands, and even our hips and legs. All great work. But, by the time She got down to our feet and toes, She was a little distracted and just said, Okay, there's two of them with five digits each, just like the hands, so, good enough.

This is the reason toes don't look as lovely as some other parts of the body. They're an afterthought. So we have to take care of them a little more than we might imagine. That's my story, and I'm sticking to it.

Things to remember: your face and your hands are almost always visible to others. Keep both in top form, especially in cold weather climates.

Things to avoid: revealing your bare feet to others anymore than is absolutely necessary.

THE SKIN

Description: the largest organ of your body, which holds our other vital organs in place, regulates our body temperature, and protects us from the elements.

Best practices: drinking enough water, avoiding prolonged exposure to the sun, and moisturizing with quality, organic products are three big ways to protect and nourish your skin.

The deodorant that you use is a seldom-considered but important choice that affects your skin's ability to function, and, in turn, your overall health. While deodorant does help us to, you know, *not smell bad*, it is also a product that inhibits your body's natural secretion of toxins.

In addition to inhibiting your body's natural cleansing and detoxifying process, some deodorants and antiperspirants can also release tons of harmful chemicals into your body. These include aluminum, parabens, steareths, triclosan, propylene glycol, TEA and DEA, and those always delightful 'artificial colors', which can be almost anything.

Read the labels of deodorants and antiperspirants before buying. You can also check out the *Environmental Working Group (EWG) Skin Deep Database* to learn more about these ingredients and other chemicals. Protect your body. Once again: read the labels and do your research.

Take the time to pamper your skin now in order to give the best chance of serving you well of years to come. Wear a hat if the sun is blazing. Again, keep your skin hydrated by drinking enough water each day. Exercise for blood flow. Moisturize with quality products.

Organic rosehip seed oil applied daily will greatly alleviate the appearance of wrinkles on your face. (Consult your doctor first before starting any exercise regimen or using products that may have adverse effects. If you have sensitive skin or a pre-existing skin condition, consult a dermatologist. Research skin products best for you.)

Use an aftershave lotion that hydrates (alcohol free). Use deodorants that are aluminum and paraben-free.

Preferred Products: pure Squalane Oil is great for all skin types, excellent for softening the skin and providing more skin flexibility. Grapeseed and hempseed oil help acne prone skin. Avocado oil and Marula Oil are great for dry skin. Jojoba oil and rosehip seed oil work well to combat blemishes. Sea buckthorn and rosehip seed oil are miracle workers for aging skin.

Tom's brand is the preferred deodorant. Agent Nature brand is also a premium choice.

Usually worn with: clothes.

Never worn with: tattoos, if possible. Tattoo ink can be toxic and can complicate medical procedures that may save your life in the future (MRI results). If you already have a tattoo, do some research on the health hazards of tattoo ink, and please don't get more. If you don't have one, please don't get one.

How to care for it: stay out of the sun, moisturize, avoid smoking cigarettes, and moderate alcohol intake.

Things to remember: shirts with collars and sleeves will protect the skin on your neck and arms from undue sun exposure and skin damage.

If you see a freckle or sun spot appear on your skin, keep an eye on it. If it becomes irregular in shape (not oval or round) and larger than a one-eighth of an inch in diameter, go to the doctor and have it examined. Use Tamanu oil. It will lessen the appearance of sunspots.

Things to avoid: thinking tanning booths or tanning creams are good ideas. Thinking that a sunburn is funny.

THE TEETH

Description: those pearly-whites that you smile and chew food with.

History, if you care: have been known to be very convenient when you want to eat something, very painful when they aren't healthy, and very much missed when they are gone.

Best practices: good dental hygiene. That's the best practice there is. The old cliches of brushing a few times a day, flossing, and visiting the dentist regularly will serve you well.

To straighten teeth, explore affordable orthodontic options.

Note that you can't really have a fabulous, Old Money Style if you don't take care of your teeth.

Things to remember: dental appointments. Mouthwash. Breath mints.

Things to avoid: gold grills. Fake-looking veneers.

Part IV

Style and Substance

GOING FORWARD

Although we've reached the end of this book, it's just the beginning for you. That's why this chapter is entitled 'Going Forward' and not 'Conclusion'.

You've been exposed to some direction, some guidelines, some examples, some vendors, some perspective, and some philosophy.

Plato said, *Learning is remembering.* For education to have any value, we must remember it. So, the time has come for you to consider what you've read, determine how to integrate it into your life, and remember it.

Notice I didn't say, *consider how you're going to change your wardrobe.* Your clothing is an important but arguably superficial aspect of your life. Again, with enough money, you can change your clothes in a matter of minutes. Changing your priorities, your habits, and your values requires awareness, perseverance, and eternal vigilance. It is easier when you are young, but it is never really easy.

And, truthfully, that is what this book has really been all about: how to take the concepts of reliability, honesty, valor, and modesty, and, like the wardrobe designer of a film, conceptualize and assemble them into a visual format that can be efficiently implemented by you and quickly understood by others.

This sartorial construct will first influence and perhaps persuade others that you have the above-mentioned virtues. It will, again, be up to you to follow through, to make the performance equal or superior to the presentation.

What I have provided here is a way for you to clear that first hurdle: the first impression.

These fundamentals of clothing will, over time, influence your behavior. You will, as Napoleon remarked, become a creature of your uniform.

You will, however, need to learn and experience more. You will need to become familiar with the rules of etiquette, pick up a second language, travel, and read broadly. You will need to mold and shape yourself into a gentleman.

Just as Old Money families direct and shape generation after generation in order

. grow the family's fortune and reputation, I have tried to mold the
_e yourself, the belief you have in yourself, and what you see as possible
urself.

I sincerely hope that you will benefit from the information and wisdom I've shared
in this book. It is my hope that you will define what success is for you, and that
you achieve it.

Yes, create wealth. Provide products with value and offer world-class service.
Employ and empower people. Be the 'founding father' of your dynasty. Then pass
on the Core Values I present in The Old Money Book to the people you care
about.

If you are already affluent, consider what you owe society. If you were born into
an affluent family, you're lucky. Don't have any illusions about it. If you have made
your own money, you have done it as a result of the brave, selfless acts of those
who have come before.

So, yes, men of means, you owe. Consider the tremendous benefits and freedoms
you enjoy. Consider how you might give back to the society that has so richly
rewarded you and your family.

People like George Washington, Sitting Bull, Thomas Jefferson, and Martin Luther
King, Jr. laid their lives and fortunes on the line to create a place where people
could be free, reach their full potential, grow rich, and not have to worry about
being murdered or thrown in jail by tyrants. *It ain't like that everywhere, pal.*

Nobody's a self made man. Shove that myth in the back of your sock drawer. Every
enduring financial success has happened in an environment blessed with political
stability, a measure of regulation, access to capital and labor, natural resources, the
free flow of information, and customers with enough money to buy what you're
selling.

Those vital ingredients are most often present in a society with the right mix of
political structures and cultural mores. And that doesn't happen by accident. It
doesn't happen overnight. And it doesn't happen without sacrifice.

To create and preserve this unique environment, someone has to constantly step up and do the right thing. It's a simple as that. And it might as well be you.

We don't need another lobbyist representing moneyed interests. We don't need another elected official facilitating the corporate agenda. We don't need somebody who's just in it—whatever 'it' is—for themselves.

We need intelligent, seasoned, and reasonable leaders who can balance the needs of entrepreneurs who provide jobs and create wealth with the rights of the employees who help them create wealth, and assistance to those less fortunate who genuinely need society's help for a period of time, or for a lifetime.

We need leaders who see the value in education, in healthcare, and who have a sense of duty to their country above all else. Especially above personal gain. Especially above mere profit.

There must come a time when the most fortunate people say, 'I have enough money. Now I need to help others.' Not with handouts, but with resources like good schools, access to medical care, and fair public policies.

There must be a time when the comfortable people say, 'I don't need to show everyone how rich I am, how different and special I am, and how much I can get away with. I need to show everyone how much we have in common and how we should all behave.'

In the past, we have been lucky to have scions of prominent families step into the public arena to do their duty: members of the Adams family from Boston, the Roosevelt family from upstate New York, the Rochon family of Louisiana, the Kennedy family from Massachusetts, and the Bush family from Texas, just to name a few. While we may agree or disagree with the particulars of their politics, we cannot discount their commitment to public service.

These examples can inform, instruct, and even inspire us. We must remember, though, that the culture from which they came embodies more than just a certain style of dress. It requires an awareness of principles and the courage to put those principles into action. For it is action that gives life, breath, and meaning to our beliefs.

173

...d act with integrity. Not only when it is convenient, but when it is ...ot only when the outcome is obvious or certain, but when it is unclear ...nown. Not only when it surely benefits us, but when it might cost us dearly.

This is patriotism. This is chivalry. This is nobility in its highest form. This is accepting the obligation of privilege: to preserve democracy and protect the vulnerable.

This, if we are to understand the concept fully, is Old Money Style: doing our duty, to the best of our ability, without consideration of recognition or reward, for the greater good, for a higher purpose. Whether it be a simple kindness for the next door neighbor or a great sacrifice for the next generation, it is what we can do. What we must do.

Let us dress well. Let us do our duty. Let us leave this world a better place than we found it.

Plus est en vous.

A FINAL THOUGHT

The work on clothes has ended. Now, I'd like to share a final thought on the substance of Old Money Style.

First, don't think that I, as the author, know it all and haven't made mistakes. I have wasted money and made poor wardrobe choices. Feel free not to emulate.

Instead, learn from my mistakes before you endeavor to make your own. Heed the advice in this book. Do not try to reinvent the wheel.

It may be tempting to rush out and buy all the garments we've discussed, all at once. Don't. Take your time. Implement these ideas gradually.

If you're starting college or a new job, make sure you've got your blue blazer, a few dress shirts, and the dress or casual pants. Topped off with a pair of brown shoes, you'll be in good shape to get started.

Most importantly, if you're going to dress like an Old Money Guy, then, damn it, act like an Old Money Guy. The world has enough posers and jerks. What we need is a few more gentlemen who embody Old Money Style. By now, you surely know that it's not just about the clothes.

If you aren't clear as to what it is about—or want to remember what it's all about—transcribe the following list onto a small piece of paper. Tape the list to your mirror. Read it each morning as you get dressed.

Like many things Old Money, it's referred to as 'style' but it's really about 'substance'. Without it, you're just changing your clothes. With it, you're changing your life.

THE PILLARS OF
⅃LD MONEY STYLE & SUBSTANCE

Study.

Work hard.

Be polite to strangers.

Be loyal to friends.

Be hard on yourself.

Be patient with others.

Do your best.

Let your actions speak loudest.

Ask questions and listen.

Read and think.

Acknowledge differences.

Don't judge.

Empathize.

Demand fairness.

Exhibit sportsmanship.

Be certain to live for something.

Be willing to die for something.

Have fun.

Love.

Made in United States
Orlando, FL
23 February 2023

30316471R00109